Parish

Our Sunday Visitor

Curriculum Division

www.osvcurriculum.com

The Subcommittee on the Catechism, United States Conference of Catholic Bishops, has found this catechetical series, © 2009 Edition, to be in conformity with the *Catechism of the Catholic Church.*

Nihil Obstat
Rev. Richard L. Schaefer

Imprimatur
✠ Most Rev. Thomas Wenski
Bishop of Orlando
December 14, 2007

The Imprimatur is an official declaration that a book or pamphlet is free of doctrinal or moral error. No implication is contained therein that anyone who granted the Imprimatur agrees with the contents, opinions, or statements expressed.

Write:
Our Sunday Visitor Curriculum Division
Our Sunday Visitor, Inc.
200 Noll Plaza, Huntington, Indiana 46750

For permission to reprint copyrighted material, grateful acknowledgment is made to the following sources:

Carolrhoda Books, Inc., a division of Lerner Publishing Group: Adapted from *Keep the Lights Burning, Abbie* (Retitled: "Abbie's Light") by Peter and Connie Roop. Text copyright 1985 by Carolrhoda Books, Inc., a division of Lerner Publishing Group.

Confraternity of Christian Doctrine, Washington, D.C.: Scriptures from the *New American Bible*. Text copyright © 1991, 1986, 1970 by the Confraternity of Christian Doctrine. All rights reserved. No part of the *New American Bible* may be used or reproduced in any form, without permission in writing from the copyright owner.

GRM Associates, Inc. on behalf of the Estate of Ida M. Cullen: From "The Wakeupworld" (Retitled: "Song of the Wake-Up-World") in *On These I Stand* by Countee Cullen. Text copyright © 1940 by Harper & Brothers; text copyright renewed © 1968 by Ida M. Cullen.

Hope Publishing Co., Carol Stream, IL 60188: Lyrics from "We Are the Church" by Richard Avery and Donald Marsh. Lyrics © 1972 by Hope Publishing Co. Lyrics from "Spirit-Friend" by Tom Colvin. Lyrics © 1969 by Hope Publishing Co.

Integrity Media, Inc., 1000 Cody Road, Mobile, AL 36695: Lyrics from "The Servant Song" by Richard Gillard. Lyrics © 1977 by Scripture In Song (c/o Integrity Music) /ASCAP.

The English translation of the Psalm Responses from *Lectionary for Mass* © 1969, 1981, 1997, International Commission on English in the Liturgy Corporation (ICEL); the English translation of the Act of Contrition from *Rite of Penance* © 1974, ICEL; the English translation of the Prayer to the Holy Spirit, Prayer to the Guardian Angel, and *Angelus* from *A Book of Prayers* © 1982, ICEL; the English translation of the Prayer after Meals from Book of Blessings © 1988, ICEL; excerpts from the English translation of *The Roman Missal* © 2010, ICEL. All rights reserved.

Additional acknowledgments appear on page 278.

Call to Faith Parish Grade 3 Student Edition
ISBN: 978-0-15-902276-4
Item Number: CU1372

8 9 10 015016 13 12 11
Manufactured by Webcrafters, Inc., Madison WI,
United States of America, June 2011, Job # 92520

Grade 3 Contents

Catholic Source Book

Faith in Action: Catholic Social Teaching

Leader: Make us one in your name, O Lord.
"How good it is, how pleasant
where the people dwell as one."
Psalm 133:1

All: Make us one in your name, O Lord. Amen.

Activity Let's Begin

The Year Ahead Today you are joining a new group—your third grade religion class. You have many exciting things to look forward to this year. You will meet new people and learn new things. You will grow closer to Jesus and the Church.

You will be learning and growing along with your classmates. You may have some new people in your class. What would you want to tell them about yourself?

What are some of your Favorite Things?

Movie

Season

Outside Activity

About Your Faith

Part of growing in faith is making new friends with people in your class and parish. Your family, friends, and parish community help you follow Jesus. With them you spend time reading from the Bible. You learn more about the Church and how to share God's love with others.

SCHOOL BUS

Activity

Share Your Faith

Think: What is your favorite Bible story?

____

____

____

Why is the story special to you?

Share: With a partner take turns talking about your favorite stories.

Act: Act out one of the stories for the class.

About Your Book

Your book will help you to learn more about your faith, important people of faith, and ways Catholics celebrate faith.

Activity Connect Your Faith

Seek and Find As you read your book, you will find lots of different things. To get to know your book better, look for the features listed below. Write down where you find each of them.

SCRIPTURE

Page ____________________

A STORY

Page ____________________

Faith Fact

Page ____________________

Words of Faith

Page ____________________

People of Faith

Page ____________________

Let Us Pray

Page ____________________

Focus

Page ____________________

A Call to Faith

Gather

Pray the Sign of the Cross together.

Leader: The Lord be with you.

All: **And with your spirit.**

Leader: Let us pray.

Bow your head as the leader prays.

All: **Amen.**

Listen to God's Word

Reader: A reading from the holy Gospel.

Read Mark 1:16–20.

The Gospel of the Lord.

All: **Praise to you, Lord Jesus Christ.**

Reflect

How do you think Jesus' first followers felt?

How do you answer Jesus' call today?

Signing of the Senses

Leader: Let us pray.

Jesus, you call us to believe in you.

All: **We believe in you.**

Trace the Sign of the Cross on your forehead.

Leader: Jesus, you call us to love you.

All: **We love you.**

Trace the Sign of the Cross on your forehead.

Leader: Jesus, you call us to share your message with others.

All: **We will tell others about you.**

Trace the Sign of the Cross on your forehead.

Leader: Glory to the Father, and to the Son, and to the Holy Spirit,

All: **As it was in the beginning, is now, and will be for ever. Amen.**

Go Forth!

Leader: Let us go forth to share the love of Christ with one another.

All: Thanks be to God.

Sing together.

We are called to act with justice,
we are called to love tenderly,
we are called to serve one another;
to walk humbly with God!

Times to Celebrate

Many families gather together for special events. Birthdays, anniversaries, and holidays are important times for families. They share stories and honor loved ones on these days.

The Church gathers for special days and times, too. These special times are called the seasons of the Church year. The Church remembers important events in the lives of Jesus, Mary, and saints.

The Church celebrates with different words and actions.

Words and Actions
Hands are raised in prayer.
The Cross is honored by kneeling in front of it or kissing it.
The sign of Christ's peace is offered with a handshake.
The Sign of the Cross is marked on foreheads, hearts, and lips.

Your class will use these words and actions to celebrate the different seasons.

The Church Year

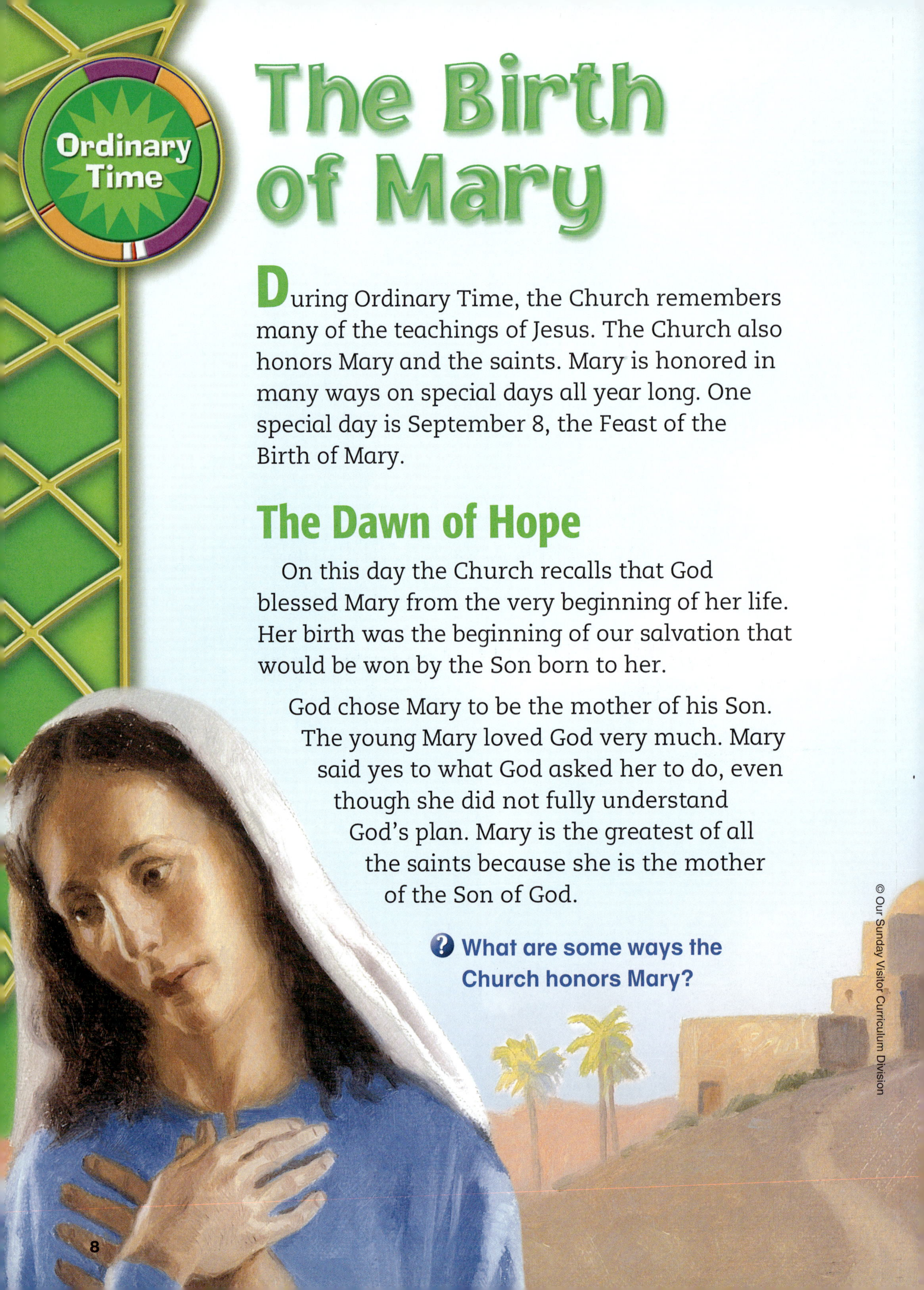

The Birth of Mary

During Ordinary Time, the Church remembers many of the teachings of Jesus. The Church also honors Mary and the saints. Mary is honored in many ways on special days all year long. One special day is September 8, the Feast of the Birth of Mary.

The Dawn of Hope

On this day the Church recalls that God blessed Mary from the very beginning of her life. Her birth was the beginning of our salvation that would be won by the Son born to her.

God chose Mary to be the mother of his Son. The young Mary loved God very much. Mary said yes to what God asked her to do, even though she did not fully understand God's plan. Mary is the greatest of all the saints because she is the mother of the Son of God.

What are some ways the Church honors Mary?

Gather

Pray the Sign of the Cross together.

Leader: Blessed be God.

All: **Blessed be God forever.**

Sing together.

And holy is your name through
all generations!
Everlasting is your mercy
to the people you have chosen,
and holy is your name.

"Holy Is Your Name" © 1989, GIA Publications, Inc.

Leader: Let us pray.

Bow your head as the leader prays.

All: **Amen.**

Listen to God's Word

Leader: A reading from the Letter to the Romans.

Read Romans 8:28–30.

The word of the Lord.

All: **Thanks be to God.**

Reflect

How was Mary part of God's purpose?

How did God glorify Mary?

Take some quiet time to think of ways God is calling you.

Litany of Mary

Kneel as the leader begins.

Leader: God our Father

All: **have mercy on us.**

Leader: God the Son

All: **have mercy on us.**

Leader: God the Holy Spirit

All: **have mercy on us.**

Leader: Holy Mary

All: **pray for us.**

Continue to respond "pray for us" as the leader reads more titles for Mary.

Leader: Pray for us, holy Mother of God.

All: **That we may become worthy of the promises of Christ.**

Go Forth!

Leader: Let us go forth to trust in God's plan as Mary did.

All: **Thanks be to God.**

Sing together.

And holy is your name through all
  generations!
Everlasting is your mercy
to the people you have chosen,
and holy is your name.

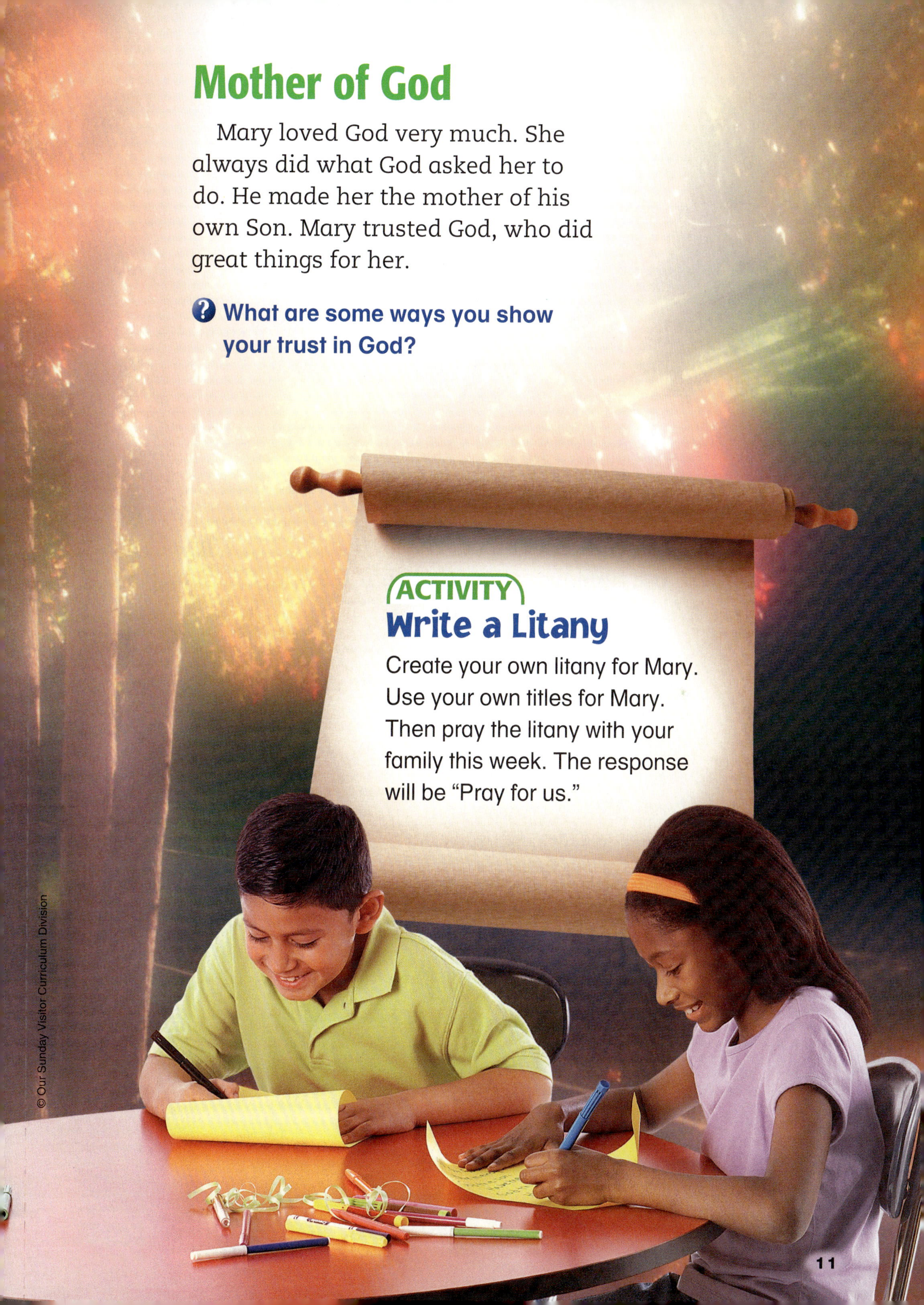

Mother of God

Mary loved God very much. She always did what God asked her to do. He made her the mother of his own Son. Mary trusted God, who did great things for her.

What are some ways you show your trust in God?

ACTIVITY

Write a Litany

Create your own litany for Mary. Use your own titles for Mary. Then pray the litany with your family this week. The response will be "Pray for us."

God's Own Light

The first season of the Church year is Advent. It is a very special time. During Advent you prepare to celebrate the birth of Jesus.

Waiting for the Light

Long before Jesus was born, God's people waited for a Savior to bring light into their lives. They "walked in darkness" (Isaiah 9:1). When the time was right, God sent his Son, God's own Light, into the world.

Advent helps you remember that Jesus is the light in your life, too. The Advent wreath reminds you to prepare your heart to welcome Jesus. The Advent wreath has four candles. A candle is lit each week during Advent. A special prayer is prayed to ask that the light of Jesus come into your life.

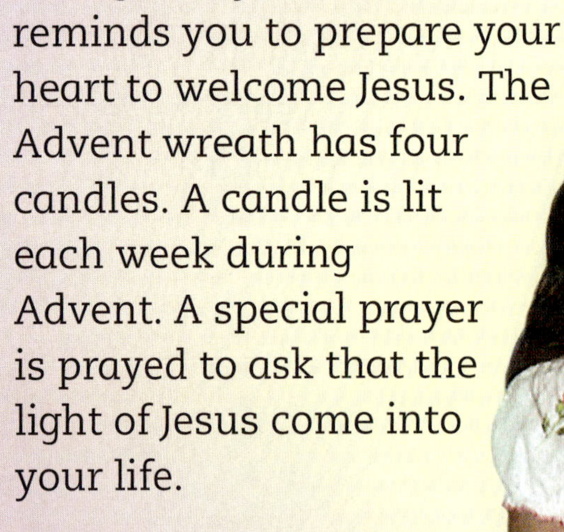

What are some things your family does during Advent?

Celebrate Advent

Gather

Pray the Sign of the Cross together.

Leader: Our help is in the name of the Lord.

All: **Who made heaven and earth.**

Sing together.

We are walking in the light,
in the light, in the light
We are walking in the light,
in the light of God.

Leader: Let us pray.

Bow your heads as the leader prays.

All: Amen.

Listen to God's Word

Reader: A reading from the holy Gospel according to John.

Read John 1:6–9.

The Gospel of the Lord.

All: **Praise to you, Lord Jesus Christ.**

Reflect

Who is Jesus?

How is Jesus a light to you?

Prayer of the Faithful

Leader: Let us pray.

Jesus, Light of the World,
we ask you to bring your healing light
to those for whom we now pray.

Respond to each prayer with these words.

All: Lord, hear our prayer.

Procession of Praise

Leader: Strengthen the hands that are feeble,
make firm the knees that are weak.

Isaiah 35:3

Process around the prayer space with arms raised.

Sing together.

We are walking in the light,
in the light, in the light
We are walking in the light,
in the light of God.

"We Are Walking in the Light" © 1987, GIA Publication, Inc.

Go Forth!

Leader: Let us go forth this week to prepare
our hearts to welcome Jesus.

All: Thanks be to God.

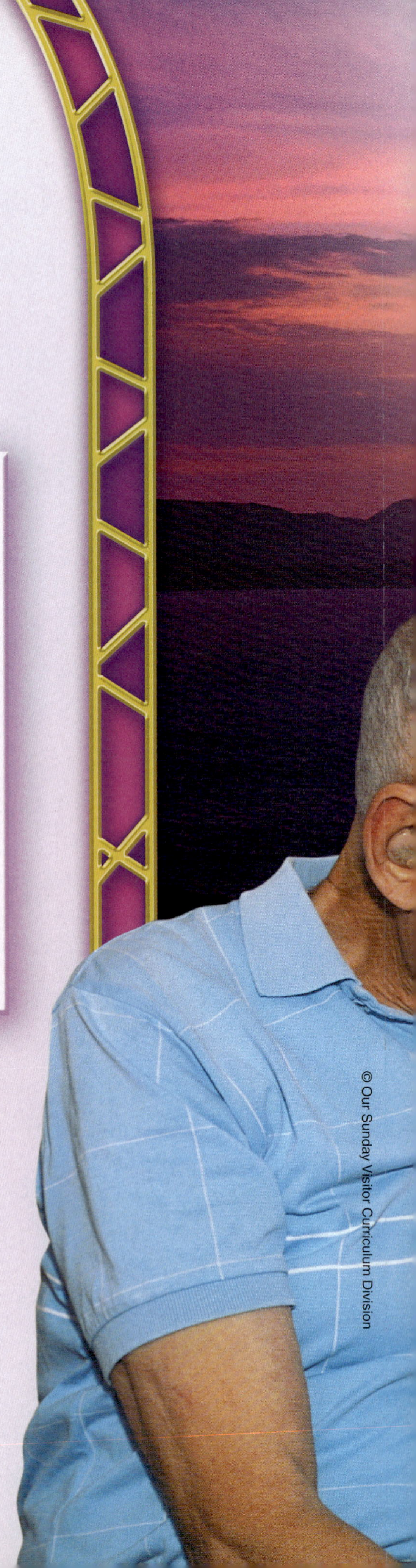

The Light of Day

John the Baptist, Jesus' cousin, helped point the way to Jesus, the Light of the World. God chose John to help others recognize Jesus. Jesus comes into the darkness and breaks it open with God's light.

How can you point others to Jesus, God's own Light?

ACTIVITY

Be Light to Others

When you follow Jesus' example, you share his light with others. How can you bring light into someone else's life? Write one thing you can do at home and one thing you do at school.

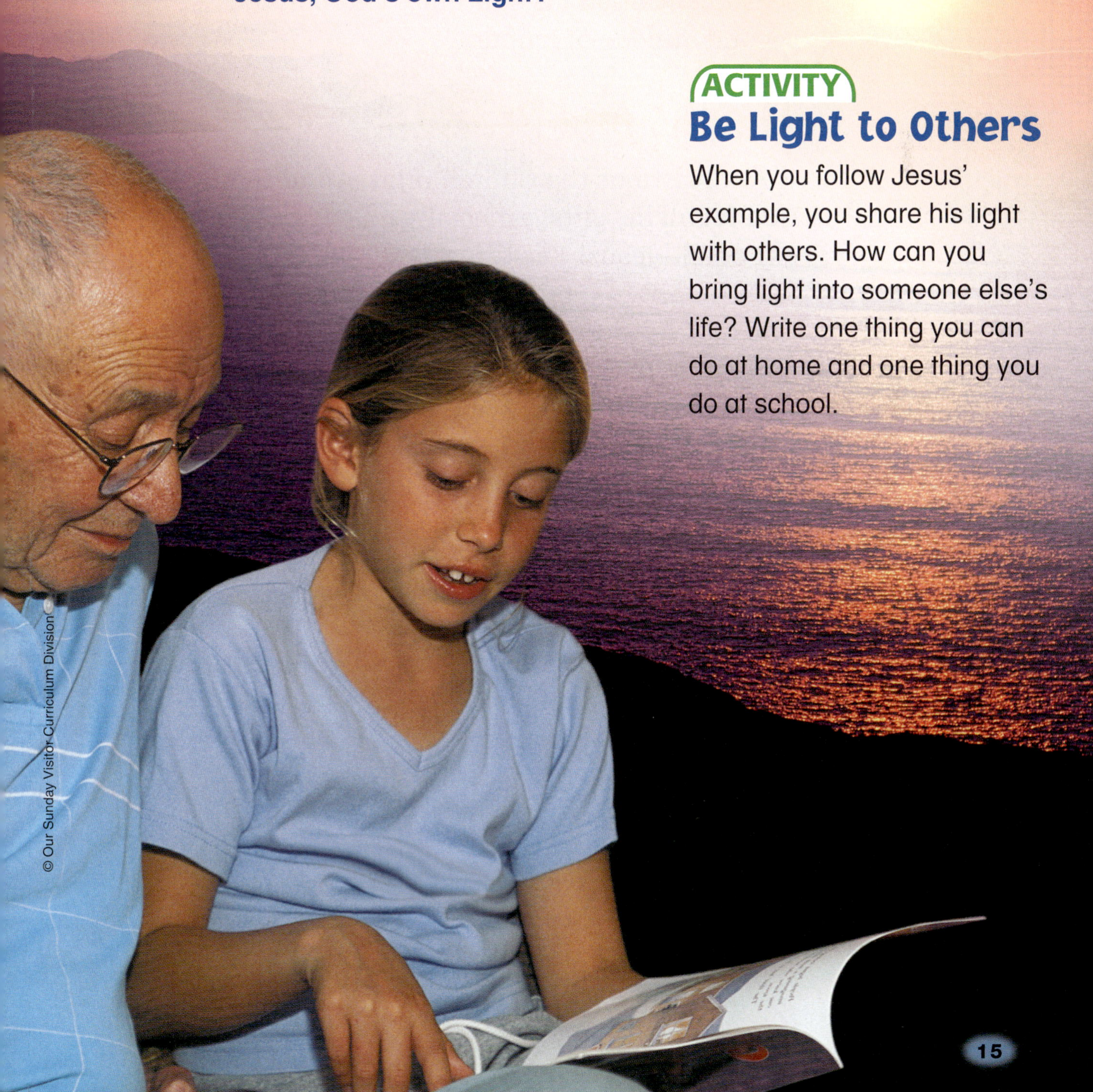

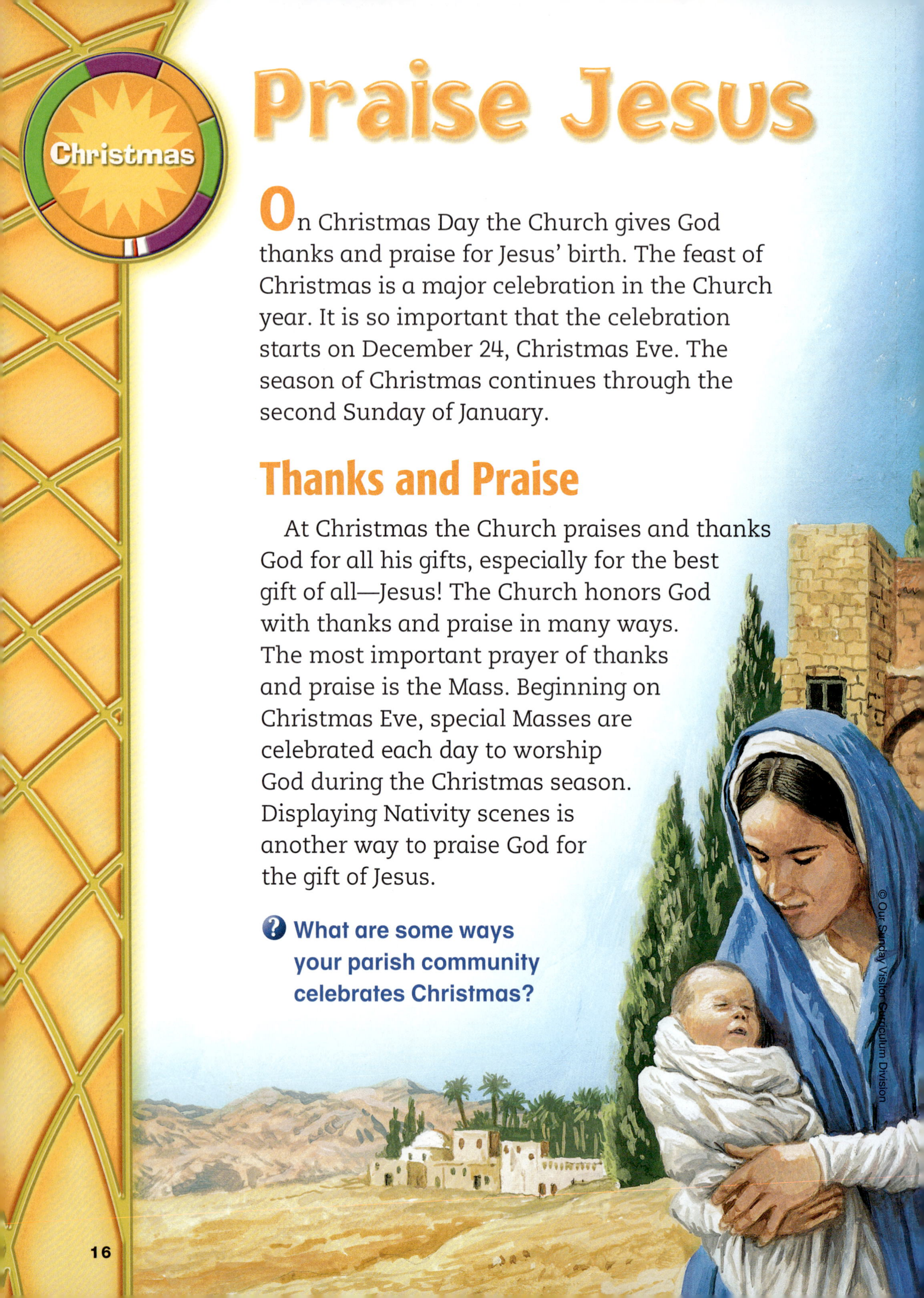

Praise Jesus

On Christmas Day the Church gives God thanks and praise for Jesus' birth. The feast of Christmas is a major celebration in the Church year. It is so important that the celebration starts on December 24, Christmas Eve. The season of Christmas continues through the second Sunday of January.

Thanks and Praise

At Christmas the Church praises and thanks God for all his gifts, especially for the best gift of all—Jesus! The Church honors God with thanks and praise in many ways. The most important prayer of thanks and praise is the Mass. Beginning on Christmas Eve, special Masses are celebrated each day to worship God during the Christmas season. Displaying Nativity scenes is another way to praise God for the gift of Jesus.

What are some ways your parish community celebrates Christmas?

Celebrate Jesus

Gather

Sing together the refrain.

Go tell it on the mountain,
Over the hills and ev'rywhere;
Go tell it on the mountain
That Jesus Christ is born!

Pray the Sign of the Cross together.

Leader: Blessed be the name of the Lord.

All: Now and for ever.

Leader: Let us pray.

Bow your heads as you praise God.

All: Amen.

Listen to God's Word

Leader: A reading from the holy Gospel according to Luke.

Read Luke 2:1–14.

The Gospel of the Lord.

All: Praise to you, Lord Jesus Christ.

Reflect

What parts of the Christmas celebration are special for you?

How do you celebrate Christmas with your family?

The Lord's Prayer and Sign of Peace

Leader: At the Savior's command, we dare to say:

All: **Our Father . . .**

Leader: May the God of light and peace fill our hearts and lives.

All: **Amen.**

Leader: Let us offer each other the sign of peace.

Offer one another a Sign of Peace.

Go Forth!

Leader: Let us go forth this week to give thanks for God's gift of Jesus.

All: **Thanks be to God.**

Sing together the refrain.

Go tell it on the mountain,
Over the hills and ev'rywhere;
Go tell it on the mountain
That Jesus Christ is born!

God's Great Gift

God gives you a special gift in Jesus. You can give your own gifts to God. Your prayers of thanksgiving are your gifts. You can pray with words, gestures, and actions, during the Mass or at any time.

What is your favorite way to thank and praise God in prayer?

Have you seen other people pray in ways that are different from the way you pray?

ACTIVITY

Start a Prayer Journal

Share your thoughts and feelings with God. Do this for a week. You might find yourself liking it and may even want to continue doing it after the week is up.

Sharing God's Word

During Ordinary Time, many feasts of saints are celebrated. One such feast is February 14 (May 11 in the East) when the lives of Saints Cyril and Methodius are remembered. The Church recalls how these brothers brought God's word to the people of Eastern Europe.

Saints Cyril and Methodius

Cyril and Methodius lived hundreds of years ago in Greece. Cyril was a librarian. Methodius was a teacher at a university. Then God called Cyril and Methodius to become priests.

Later the brothers went to a country in Eastern Europe. There were no Bibles or other books in Slavonic, the local language. Slavonic had no written alphabet.

Cyril created an alphabet for Slavonic, and together he and Methodius translated the Bible and other books used at Mass. At last the people could read God's word!

Who helps you read God's word in the Bible?

Celebrate God's Word

Gather

Sing together.

We are sent, two by two.
Sent as church in the world.
Sent to share God's good news,
Sing and tell, spread the Word.

Pray the Sign of the Cross together.

Leader: Our help is in the name of the Lord.

All: **Who made heaven and earth.**

Leader: Let us pray.

Bow your heads as the leader prays.

All: **Amen.**

Listen to God's Word

Leader: A reading from the prophet Jeremiah.

Read Jeremiah 1:4–9.

The word of the Lord.

All: **Thanks be to God.**

Signing of Foreheads

Silently pray asking the Holy Spirit to strengthen you to share God's word with all you meet.

Then come forward as your name is called. The leader will mark your forehead with the Sign of the Cross.

Leader: (Name), may your words and actions bring the good news of Jesus to others.

All: Amen.

Prayer of the Faithful

Leader: Let us pray. We are called to share your word. Hear our prayers for strength.

Respond to each prayer with these words.

All: Lord, send us to share your word.

Leader: At the Savior's command, we dare to say:

All: Our Father . . .

Go Forth!

Leader: Let us go forth to share God's word with everyone we meet this week.

All: Thanks be to God.

God's Word to Others

God may never ask you to go to a distant country to share his word as he asked Cyril and Methodius to do. But God asks each follower of Jesus to bring his word to their families, friends, neighbors, and classmates. And God may someday call you to be a missionary in a faraway place.

What are ways that others have shared God's word with you?

ACTIVITY

Teach the Word

This week, think of yourself as someone teaching the word of God in your own family, neighborhood, or school. What will you do to share God's word with someone?

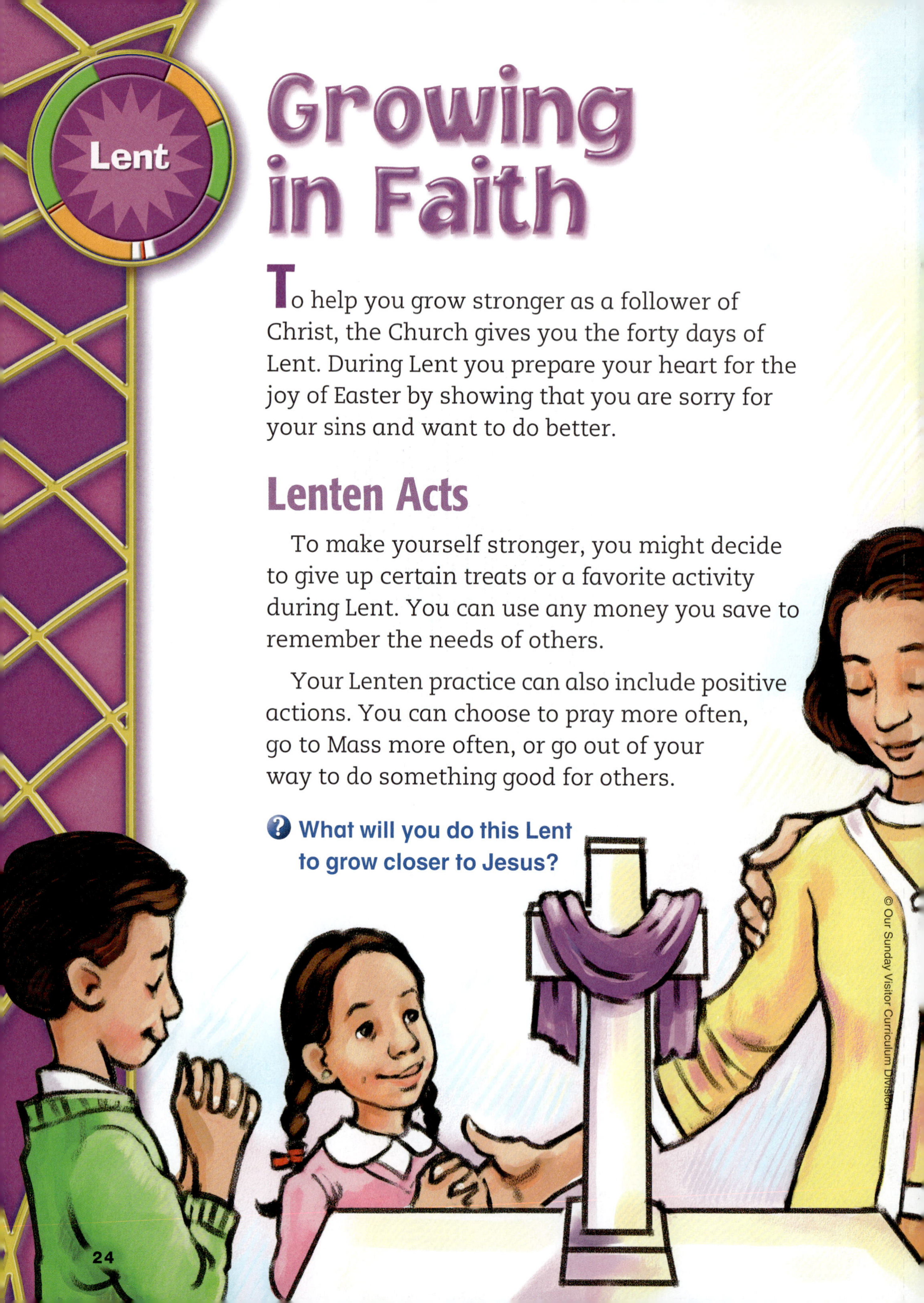

Growing in Faith

To help you grow stronger as a follower of Christ, the Church gives you the forty days of Lent. During Lent you prepare your heart for the joy of Easter by showing that you are sorry for your sins and want to do better.

Lenten Acts

To make yourself stronger, you might decide to give up certain treats or a favorite activity during Lent. You can use any money you save to remember the needs of others.

Your Lenten practice can also include positive actions. You can choose to pray more often, go to Mass more often, or go out of your way to do something good for others.

What will you do this Lent to grow closer to Jesus?

Celebrate Lent

Gather

Pray the Sign of the Cross together.

Leader: O Lord, open my lips.

All: **That my mouth shall proclaim your praise.**

Leader: Let us pray.

Bow your heads as the leader prays.

All: **Amen.**

Listen to God's Word

Leader: A reading from the letter to the Ephesians.

Read Ephesians 5:1–2, 8–10.

The word of the Lord.

All: **Thanks be to God.**

Reflect

What does it mean to be a child of God?

How can you be a light to others?

Silent Prayer

Sit in silence before the cross with your eyes downcast or closed. Ask God to be with you. Think about what you can do during Lent to grow stronger as a follower of Jesus.

Prayer of the Faithful

Leader: Let us pray. Lord Jesus, you promise that God, our Father, will hear our prayers. We pray those prayers now.

Respond to each prayer with these words.

All: **Lord, hear our prayer.**

Leader: At the Savior's command, we dare to say:

All: **Our Father . . .**

Sing together.

Peace before us, peace behind us,
peace under our feet.
Peace within us, peace over us,
let all around us be peace.

Continue to sing verse beginning with "Love" and then "Light."

Go Forth!

Leader: Let us go forth this week to share Christ's light and peace with those around us.

All: **Thanks be to God.**

More Like Jesus

The cross is the sign of what Jesus was willing to do for all people. Making the Sign of the Cross is a reminder that you belong to Jesus. During Lent you and your faith community strive to become more like Jesus through prayer and helping others.

Who reminds you most of Jesus?

How are you "Jesus" for others each day?

ACTIVITY

Make a Lenten Cross

Make a cross from scrap materials you find around the house. You may choose to write Lenten words on it, such as *prayer, self-giving,* or *Jesus.* Hang your cross in a place where it will remind you often of the extra things you are doing during Lent.

Rejoice!

At the end of Lent, the Church remembers and celebrates what Jesus did for all people. The Church calls these three special days the Triduum. The Triduum begins at the Holy Thursday Mass of the Lord's Supper and ends with evening prayer on Easter Sunday.

The Three Days

On Holy Thursday the Church recalls Jesus' Last Supper with his disciples. On Good Friday Jesus' suffering and death on the cross is remembered. Holy Saturday is a day of prayerful waiting to celebrate Jesus' Resurrection.

The liturgy on Holy Saturday evening is called the Easter Vigil. The word vigil means "keeping watch by night." At the Easter Vigil the Church community keeps watch with those waiting to be baptized.

To express the joy of Jesus' Resurrection, the deacon or other minister sings the Easter Proclamation.

What are some other ways people express joy in the Resurrection?

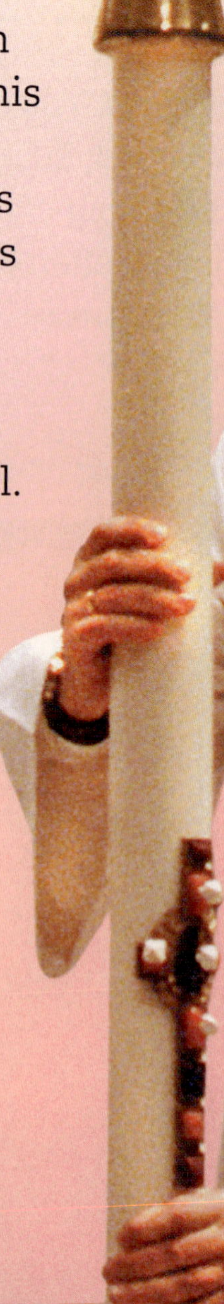

Celebrate the Three Days

Gather

Sing together.

O how good is Christ the Lord!
On the cross he died for me.
In three days he rose again.
Glory be to Jesus!
Glory be to Jesus! Glory be to Jesus!
In three days he rose again.
Glory be to Jesus!

Pray the Sign of the Cross together.

Leader: O Lord, open my lips.

All: **That my mouth shall proclaim your praise.**

Leader: Let us pray.

Bow your heads as the leader prays.

All: **Amen.**

Listen to God's Word

Reader: A reading from the Letter to the Romans.

Read Romans 6:3–5.

The word of the Lord.

All: **Thanks be to God.**

Reflect

How do you feel about sharing in Jesus' new life through Baptism?

How can you live the new life Jesus won for you?

Remember Baptism

Leader: Let us renew the promises made at Baptism.

Respond "I do" to the leader's questions.

Go Forth!

Leader: Let us go forth this week to remember and celebrate Jesus' great love for us.

All: **Thanks be to God.**

Sing together.

O how good is Christ the Lord!
On the cross he died for me.
In three days he rose again.
 Glory be to Jesus!
Glory be to Jesus! Glory be to Jesus!
In three days he rose again.
 Glory be to Jesus!

"O How Good Is Christ the Lord" © 2000, GIA Publications, Inc.

Baptismal Promises

When you were baptized, your parents probably made the baptismal promises for you. Now that you are older, you can make those same promises for yourself. During the Easter Vigil you will renew your baptismal promises with the whole community. These promises show you are a follower of Jesus.

How do you show that you are a follower of Jesus?

ACTIVITY

Make Promises

Work with a partner. Make a list of things your class can do to show you are followers of Jesus. Begin each with "We will . . ." Then make a banner of class promises.

Holy, Holy, Holy

On Easter day, the holiest day of the Church year, the Church celebrates Jesus being raised from the dead. It celebrates the everlasting life that is yours because of Jesus' death and Resurrection. Every Sunday is called the Lord's Day because that is the day Jesus rose from the dead.

A Holy People

To be holy means to be like God. God made all people to be like himself. He wants everyone to be holy. By his death, Jesus made people holy, again. Through the waters of Baptism, Christians share in the life and holiness Jesus won for them.

At Easter Mass the assembly renews the promises made when they were baptized. The priest walks throughout the church and sprinkles everyone with the holy water that was blessed at the Easter Vigil.

Where is the holy water in your parish church? When do you use it?

Celebrate Easter

Gather

Sing together.

New beginnings, here in our midst:
 Alleluia! Alleluia!
We are God's children, holy and blest:
 Alleluia! Alleluia!
People of God, rejoice and sing!
Alleluia! Alleluia! Alleluia! Alleluia!

Pray the Sign of the Cross together.

Leader: Light and peace in Jesus Christ our Lord, Alleluia.

All: **Thanks be to God, Alleluia.**

Leader: Let us pray.

Bow your heads as the leader prays.

All: **Amen.**

Sprinkling Rite

Leader: With joy you will draw water joyfully at the fountain of salvation.

Isaiah 12:3

All: **This is the day the Lord has made; let us rejoice in it and be glad.**

Psalm 118:24

As the leader sprinkles you with holy water, make the Sign of the Cross and recall that you are a child of God.

Listen to God's Word

Reader: A reading from the holy Gospel according to Luke.

Read Luke 24:1–12.

The Gospel of the Lord.

All: **Praise to you, Lord Jesus Christ.**

Reflect

Imagine that you are at Jesus' tomb. What might you say or do?

Prayer of the Faithful

Leader: Let us pray. Jesus, you were raised from the dead so that we might live as a holy people. Listen to our loving prayers.

Respond to each prayer with these words.

All: **Lord, hear our prayer.**

Leader: At the Savior's command, we dare to say:

All: **Our Father . . .**

Go Forth!

Leader: Let us go to live as holy people who belong to the Risen Jesus, Alleluia, Alleluia.

All: **Thanks be to God, Alleluia, Alleluia.**

Living Water

During the Easter season, the assembly gathered is sprinkled with holy water. This is a reminder of the importance of Baptism. Through Baptism you share in the new life of Jesus who is risen forever.

Who are some people in your life who live as holy people?

ACTIVITY

Present an Easter Play

Together with your classmates, act out the events of the first Easter morning. Use your own words, and wear simple costumes if you wish. Your class might like to present this as a play for a group of younger children.

The Holy Spirit

The Church celebrates Pentecost fifty days after Easter. This great feast celebrates the coming of the Holy Spirit upon Jesus' first disciples. The assembly prays for the Holy Spirit to come to them, too.

Sharing the Holy Spirit

After Jesus returned to his Father, the disciples did not know what to do. Then, as Jesus had promised, The Holy Spirit was sent to them.

The Holy Spirit strengthened the disciples. With his help, they shared the good news of Jesus with everyone they met.

The good news that Jesus shared was that everyone is welcome in his Father's kingdom. Jesus also taught that God's kingdom is one of peace, justice, and love.

The Holy Spirit gives us the power to share the good news of God's kingdom with everyone we meet.

What is some good news about Jesus that you can share?

Celebrate the Holy Spirit

Gather

Sing together.

God sends us his Spirit to befriend
and help us.
Recreate and guide us, Spirit-Friend
Spirit who enlivens, sanctifies, enlightens,
Sets us free, is now our Spirit-Friend.
Spirit of our Maker, Spirit-Friend.

Pray the Sign of the Cross together.

Leader: Light and peace in Jesus Christ our Lord, Alleluia.

All: **Thanks be to God, Alleluia.**

Leader: Let us pray.

Bow your heads as the leader prays.

All: **Amen.**

Listen to God's Word

Honoring the Scriptures

Leader: Come, Holy Spirit, fill the hearts of your faithful.

All: **And kindle in them the fire of your love.**

Kneel as the Bible is carried to the prayer table. When the Bible is placed on its stand, take turns respectfully bowing in front of it.

Leader: A reading from the Acts of the Apostles.

Read Acts 2:1–11.

The word of the Lord.

All: **Thanks be to God.**

Reflect

In the story of the first Pentecost, what was the coming of the Holy Spirit like?

What signs of the Holy Spirit are in the world today?

Prayer of the Faithful

Leader: Let us pray. God the Holy Spirit, you fill us with your power and strength. Hear the prayers that we bring to you now.

Respond to each prayer with these words.

All: **Hear our prayer, O Lord.**

Leader: Let us offer praise to the Holy Trinity.

All: **Glory to the Father . . .**

Go Forth!

Leader: Let us go forth this week to share God's word with everyone we meet.

All: **Thanks be to God.**

The Power of the Holy Spirit

The Feast of Pentecost celebrates the gift of the Holy Spirit to all Christ's followers. With the Holy Spirit's guidance and strength, you can follow Christ and work for God's kingdom of justice, love, and peace.

How can young people show others how to follow Christ?

ACTIVITY

Signs of Peace

What are some signs of peace and justice in your parish, your school, your country? With a partner make of lists of some of these signs. Choose one thing you can do to spread peace and love.

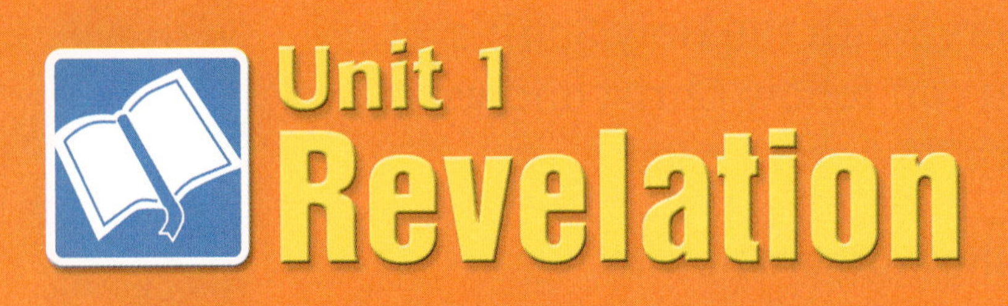

In this unit you will...

learn that all of creation shows God's plan of goodness. You are part of God's plan. We discover God's plan in the Bible. Our families show us God's love and his plan for us. We also learn about God's plan for the Church, the People of God.

What do you think you will learn in this unit about the family of God?

Chapter 1

God's Beautiful World

Leader: God our Creator, we praise your beautiful creation!

"Let them all praise the LORD's name;
for the LORD's commanded and
they were created."

Psalm 148:5

All: God our Creator, we praise your beautiful creation! Amen.

Activity Let's Begin

Song of the Wake-Up-World

Wake up, O World; O World, awake!
The light is bright on hill and lake;
O World, awake; wake up, O World!
The flags of the wind are all unfurled;
Wake up, O World; O World, awake!
Of earth's delightfulness partake.

A selection from the poem by Countee Cullen

- What beauty have you seen in God's world today?

Explore

Learning from the Past

What are some of God's gifts?

Here is a story of how one family learned about family members of long ago.

A STORY

Gifts from the Past

"Wow, what an old house!" said Seth.

"My great-grandfather built it long ago," Mom said. "My grandfather and father grew up in it."

Aunt Martha welcomed Seth's family into her home. Mom looked around. "Oh, I had forgotten how beautiful Grandma's quilts are. Grandma used pieces from worn-out clothes to make the prettiest, warmest blankets I can remember."

Later the family walked through the barn. "Look at those beams," Dad said to Mom. "You can still see the marks from your great-grandfather's ax. He put so much love and care into his work."

"This is interesting," Katie said. "I know the people better because I can see what they made."

What did the children in this family learn about their ancestors?

Learning from Creation

Katie and Seth learned about their family by seeing what family members had made. You can learn about God through his creation. God used his power to **create** everything that exists.

Words of Faith

To **create** means to make something completely new. Only God can create something where nothing existed before.

SCRIPTURE — Genesis 1:1—2:3

The Creation of the Earth

On the first day God made light. He separated the light from the darkness and called them day and night.

On the second day God separated the sky from the water below.

On the third day God separated the land from the water. He made plants and trees.

On the fourth day God made the moon, the sun, and the stars and put them in the sky.

On the fifth day God made fish and birds.

On the sixth day God made land animals. Then God made man and woman in his image and likeness. He blessed them and put them in charge of everything he had created. And God saw that his creation was good.

On the seventh day God rested.

Based on *Genesis 1:1—2:3*

Activity — Share Your Faith

Think: What do you think is God's greatest creation?

Share: Talk about God's creations with your group.

Act: Draw a picture of one of God's creations to share with the class.

The Beauty of the Creator

What is the purpose of God's creation?

The Holy Trinity—Father, Son, and Spirit—worked as one to create the world. The Holy Trinity continues to care for and support creation. Everything God created is good and can tell you something about the love of the Trinity. You can come to know God through the beauty of creation. You can learn the truth of his goodness.

Everything in God's creation has a purpose. God wants all parts of his creation to live together in peace.

God's creation includes whales and hummingbirds, lightning and wind, sunshine and rain, and all people of every color. All these differences make God's world more beautiful and teach you more about his greatness.

What are some signs of God's goodness that you see around you?

In God's Image

God created humans in his own image and likeness and asked them to care for all creation. God wants you to live in his friendship and to be happy with him. You have a **responsibility** to show respect and love for God's creation.

There is also sin in the world, and because of this God's creation sometimes gets out of balance. God relies on humans to help bring back the harmony, or balance and peacefulness, that he put into his creation.

Words of Faith

A **responsibility** is a duty or a job that you are trusted to do. God gives humans the responsibility of caring for his creation.

Blessed Ones of God

Your most important responsibility in caring for creation is to the human community. Humans are the most blessed of all God's creatures. God wants you to show respect and love for all people because he created each of them in his own image. In God's community of love, everyone is your brother or sister. In your unity you can be a sign of God's goodness and love.

Activity Connect Your Faith

Show Your Uniqueness Work in groups of four. Below each fingerprint shape, write one way in which each of you is different and one way in which you are all similar.

Prayer of Praise

Gather and begin with the Sign of the Cross.

Sing together the refrain.

Alleluia.

Leader: Loving God, help us appreciate the marvelous gift of this world that you have created.

All: **We thank you, God, for the gift of creation. And so we sing.**

Sing the refrain.

Leader: You made each of us wonderfully special.

All: **We thank you, God, for the gift of creation. And so we sing.**

Sing the refrain.

Leader: Dear God, help us love your creation.

All: **Amen.**

Leader: Let us pray.

Bow your heads as the leader prays.

All: **Amen.**

The Church Community

Leader: Lord, we want to live in your presence.
"Happy are those who dwell in your house!
They never cease to praise you."
Psalm 84:5

All: Lord, we want to live in your presence. Amen.

Invite

Activity Let's Begin

Here's the Church Megan was teaching her younger friend Emily a rhyme she had learned when she was Emily's age. "It's easy," she told Emily. "Just do this." She folded her hands a certain way.

"Here's the church.
Here's the steeple.
Open the doors,
And see all the people."

"Let me try!" said Emily.

- What different people do you see when you open the doors to your church?

We Need One Another

Focus Where do you learn what God wants you to do?

Buildings are not as important as the people in them. Long ago, the people in a farming town had forgotten how important each person was to the town. They had also forgotten how to get along with one another.

A STORY

Soup for All

Clang, clang, clang! rang the bell in the town square. When the people came out to see why the bell was ringing, they met three soldiers.

"Please give us some food," the soldiers begged.

"I would like to help, but I have only carrots," said one farmer. "I must save them for my family."

"I would love to taste a carrot," said another. "My family has had only potatoes for months!"

"Carrots? Potatoes? How lucky you both are! I have only beans!" said a third farmer.

One of the soldiers clapped his hands. "I know what we can do."

What do you think happened next?

God Teaches You

The following **Bible** story tells you how God wants you to live and do his work.

The **Bible** is God's word written in human words. The Bible is the holy book of the Church.

SCRIPTURE Acts 2:42–47

Helping One Another

After the Holy Spirit came, Jesus' followers met often to learn from the Apostles, to break bread together, and to pray. Some members of the group sold what they had and gave the money to help the others. Many early Christians shared their belongings with those who were in need. These followers of Jesus were very happy, and new members joined every day.

Based on *Acts 2:42–47*

Have you ever been in a special group? How is your group like Jesus' group of followers?

Share Your Faith

Think: When have you had trouble sharing with a friend or family member?

Share: Talk to your group about how it can sometimes be difficult to share.

Act: With a partner, act out a time when you shared, even though it was difficult to do so.

Explore

People of God

Focus **Why is the Church so important?**

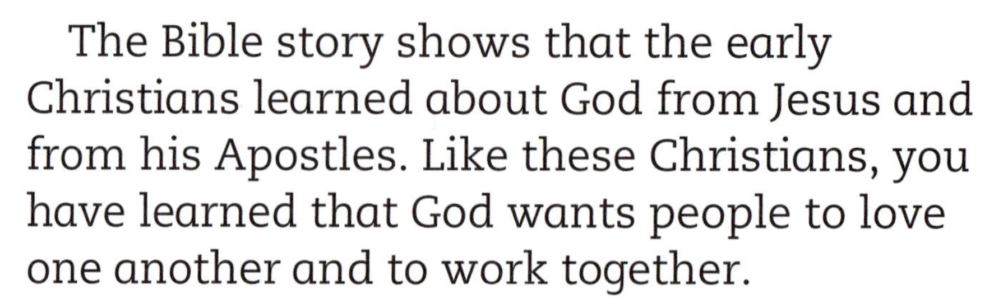

The Bible story shows that the early Christians learned about God from Jesus and from his Apostles. Like these Christians, you have learned that God wants people to love one another and to work together.

When people come together for a shared purpose, the group they form is called a *community*. God created you to be part of a community. A community can help you learn things about God that you might never know if you were learning on your own.

You feel God's love and share God's life in good communities, especially the Church. The **Church** is the People of God gathered in the name of Jesus Christ. Jesus showed all people his Father's love, and he sent the Spirit to guide the Church.

Faith Fact

The early Christians met in one another's homes because they did not have church buildings.

When do you gather with your Church community?

The Church Community

The word *church* comes from two different words. One word means "a community called together." The other word means "belonging to the Lord." These meanings tell you that the Church is different from other communities. Through Baptism, God calls you to be part of this special community gathered in Jesus' name.

Words of Faith

The **Church** is the community of the People of God gathered in the name of Jesus Christ.

As a member of the Church community, you have some very important work to do. Church members gather together to honor God and to help other people. They listen to the Church's teaching. The Church helps you understand the Bible and the message of Jesus. It teaches you about God and his love.

Activity — Connect Your Faith

God's Work What good works are the people of your parish doing? Draw one of the good works of your parish in the space below.

Prayer of Thanks

Gather and begin with the Sign of the Cross.

Reader 1: Jesus, thank you for bringing us together as a community of your followers.

All: **We join together to give you thanks.**

Reader 2: Thank you for giving us other people to help us do your work in the world.

All: **We join together to give you thanks.**

Reader 3: Help us remember that we work best when we work together.

All: **We join together to give you thanks.**

Leader: Let us pray.

Bow your heads as the leader prays.

All: **Amen.**

Sing together.

I am the church!
You are the church! We are the church together! All who follow Jesus, all around the world! Yes, we're the church together.

CHAPTER 2

Review and Apply

A Work with Words Complete each statement.

1. Some ways you learn about God are through ______________________, the Church, and the Bible.
2. A ______________________ is a group of people who come together for a shared purpose.
3. Through Baptism, God called you to be part of a special community called the ______________________.
4. The ______________________ is God's word written in human words.
5. A name for the Church community is ______________________.

B Check Understanding How did early Christians continue to follow Jesus?

____

____

Activity Live Your Faith

Draw a Poster Think of good work that needs to be done in your community. Use the space below to design a poster that invites members of your parish to help. Show people working together to get a job done.

Family Faith

Catholics Believe

- The Bible is the word of God written in human words.
- The Church is the People of God gathered in the name of Jesus.

SCRIPTURE

John 15:12–17 is about loving and caring for the Church community. Read the passage and talk about how you should love and care for one another.

GO online **www.osvcurriculum.com**
For weekly scripture readings and seasonal resources

Activity

Live Your Faith

Make a Chart Your parish is a place to worship God, to learn about God, to do works of service, and to have a good time together. Make a chart with each of these four activities. Write a way that your family can do each activity. Choose one activity that you will do to make your parish a stronger community.

▲ Saint Francis of Assisi 1182–1226

People of Faith

Francis was the son of a rich cloth merchant in Assisi, Italy. One day while Francis was praying, Jesus asked him to rebuild the Church. Francis helped people see the beauty of the world and preached the good news of Jesus to them. He lived a simple life and was kind to all creatures. His feast day is October 4. Francis is the patron saint of ecology.

Family Prayer

Saint Francis, pray for us that we may work together to build the Church. Amen.

In Unit 1 your child is learning about REVELATION.

CCC *See Catechism of the Catholic Church 781, 782 for further reading on chapter content.*

Chapter 3 At Home with God

Let Us Pray

Leader: God our Father, help us live as your people.
"How good it is, how pleasant,
where the people dwell as one!"
Psalm 133:1

All: God our Father, help us live as your people.
Amen.

Activity Let's Begin

A Family

I have a brother who likes to read,
and a sister who makes me laugh,
and a mom who gives me what I need,
and a cousin who is six and a half.

I have an aunt who visits during the year,
and a dad who comes to see me play,
and a grandmother who calls me dear,
and friends who come to my house for the day.

I have a family who loves and takes care of me.

- Who takes good care of you? Tell two good things about your father, your mother, or someone else who cares for you.

Loving One Another

How do families show their care for one another?

It is important for family members to share special times. In this story, an uncle teaches a new way to show love for others.

A STORY

Uncle Dan's Present

"Hello, everybody!" Uncle Dan said.

"Hi!" said Nathan. "What did you bring me?"

Uncle Dan looked puzzled. "I didn't bring any presents."

Nathan stomped to his room. Later, his sister Carrie knocked on his door. "Look at the birdhouse Uncle Dan and I made. We're going to make pizza next. Want to help us?"

Nathan didn't say anything. Soon he heard laughter and smelled pizza. Carrie was back at his door.

"Uncle Dan wants to teach us a card trick. Are you coming down?" she asked.

Nathan asked, "How long is he staying?"

"Only two days," Carrie replied.

What do you think Nathan will do?

Caring for One Another

Uncle Dan showed that he cared by visiting with Carrie and Nathan. Another story about a special visit is found in the Bible. This is the story of the **Visitation**.

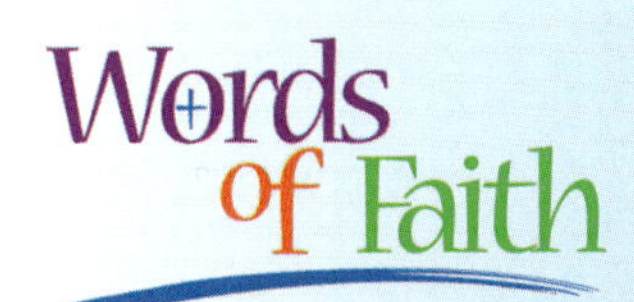

The **Visitation** is the name of the visit of Mary to Elizabeth.

SCRIPTURE Luke 1:39–56

Mary Visits Elizabeth

Mary's cousin, Elizabeth, was happy and surprised when Mary visited. Filled with the Holy Spirit, Elizabeth said to Mary, "Most blessed are you among women, and blessed is the fruit of your womb. How does this happen to me, that the mother of my Lord should come to me?"

Elizabeth's greeting made Mary happy. She answered, "My soul proclaims the greatness of the Lord; my spirit rejoices in God my savior."

Based on *Luke 1:39–56*

How did Mary and Elizabeth show that they were caring family members?

Activity Share Your Faith

Think: What is special about your family?

Share: With your group, find pictures in magazines that show ways family members can love and care for one another.

Act: Cut out and glue the pictures to a poster board.

GLUE

Explore

Families Teach Love

How is the family like the Church?

In both of the stories you just read, family members showed their love in actions and in words. You first learn about God's love for you from your family. Your family also teaches you how to love God and others.

You can learn the basics of healthy living from your family. Your family teaches you important safety rules. You may learn how to care for pets or do other chores.

Your family helps you learn prayers, such as the blessing before meals, the Lord's Prayer, and the Hail Mary. Your family introduces you to the Catholic Church. If you are baptized, you are already a member of this special family of God. The Church builds on what you have learned in your home. The family is where children first learn the lessons that the Church teaches. For this reason, the family is called the "domestic Church," or the church of the home.

What is something you have learned about the Catholic Church from your family?

Communities of Love

The church of the home can be a special sign that shows others how the three Persons of the Holy Trinity love one another. Your family can be a sign of this love, too, when you live together in faith, hope, and love.

God shares his **authority** with parents. He invites them to love and care for you just as he does. God wants you to respect the authority of your parents and others who care for you. This includes teachers and community officials. Their authority comes from God, too.

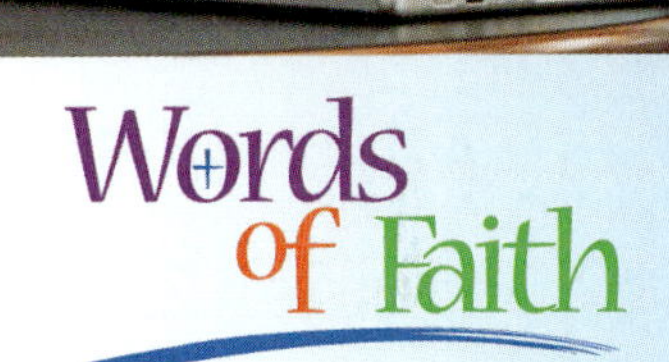

Having **authority** is being in charge of something and having the power to make decisions.

God Loves Everyone

Sometimes members of families may be busy or tired. They may let you down. They are still loved by God, just as you are. It is important to treat the members of your family with love and respect and to pray for them.

When has it been hard to obey someone who is responsible for you?

Activity — Connect Your Faith

Make a Caring Chart What words and actions show love in each of these situations? Write your ideas in each column.

Uncle Dan's Visit	The Visitation	My Family Life
grandkid	pray	watch T.V.
bird house	sing	drawing
pizza	music	church

Prayer of Thanks

Gather and begin with the Sign of the Cross.

Leader: Dear God, thank you for our families. With your help, we will try to show them our love and care.

Reader 1: When we are together,

All: **Help us show love and care.**

Reader 2: When family members are sad,

All: **Help us show love and care.**

Reader 3: When we are full of energy and ideas,

All: **Help us show love and care.**

Reader 4: When we are tired and grouchy,

All: **Help us show love and care.**

Leader: Dear God, thank you for caring families.

All: **Amen.**

Leader: Let us pray.

Bow your heads as the leader prays.

All: **Amen.**

Sing together.

All grownups, all children, all mothers, all fathers are sisters and brothers in the fam'ly of God.

Leader: Lord God, send forth the Holy Spirit to set our hearts on fire!

"The grace of the Lord Jesus Christ and the love of God and the fellowship of the holy Spirit be with all of you."

2 Corinthians 13:13

All: Lord God, send forth the Holy Spirit to set our hearts on fire! Amen.

Activity Let's Begin

Mysteries of Nature Some things in this world just can't be explained. Only God understands the mysteries of his creation.

Why did God make the sky blue and the grass green?

Why can't mud be a prettier color?

Why do insects have so many legs?

Why don't dogs meow and cats bark?

- What questions do you have about the mystery of God's creation?

Explore

Learning About Mystery

What did Saint Patrick teach about the Holy Trinity?

Have you ever learned something that was hard to understand? The story of Saint Patrick tells how the people of Ireland learned about something hard to understand.

Faith Fact

Bishop Patrick lived about 400 years after the birth of Jesus.

A STORY

Three in One

Long ago the people of Ireland had questions about God. As a bishop, Patrick was teaching about the three Persons in one God, someone asked, "How can you say that there is only one God when you pray to the Father, the Son, and the Holy Spirit?"

Patrick explained the **Holy Trinity** by plucking a shamrock from the ground. He held it up for the people to see. "The shamrock I am holding is one plant, but it has three leaves. The Father, the Son, and the Holy Spirit are not three gods. They are three Persons in one God. This is a mystery that we accept on faith."

? What helped the people better understand the mystery of the Holy Trinity ?

One God

Patrick helped the people understand that there is only one God.

You can also learn from Jesus, who told his followers about the Father and the Holy Spirit.

The **Holy Trinity** is the name for the three Persons in one God.

SCRIPTURE John 14:6–7, 16–17

The Father and the Spirit

One day Jesus was talking with his followers about God. Jesus told them, "No one comes to the Father except through me. If you know me, then you will also know my Father."

Jesus promised to ask the Father to send the Holy Spirit to teach the people.

From *John 14:6–7, 16–17*

What did Jesus say about the Father and the Spirit?

Share Your Faith

Think: Think about the Holy Trinity and the shamrock.

Share: Talk to your group about how the shamrock is like the Father, Son, and Holy Spirit.

Act: Draw a shamrock and label one leaf "Father," one leaf "Son," and one leaf "Holy Spirit."

Father, Son, and Holy Spirit

Focus **What is the work of the Trinity?**

Jesus called God "Father," and he taught his followers to call God "Father," too. By his actions Jesus showed that he is God the Son, who became human to save all people. Jesus asked his Father to send the Holy Spirit, who is God's love and grace, to be present with you.

The most important thing about the Holy Trinity is that it is a loving communion of Persons joined as one in love. The Holy Trinity is a *mystery*, a truth of faith that Catholics believe even though they cannot understand it completely. A mystery is a truth that only God can fully understand.

Through God's revelation and with his help, you can understand more about a mystery like the Trinity. You can see the Trinity at work when you see love in the world. You can see the reflection of the Trinity in the Church. You will better understand the Trinity when you see God in heaven.

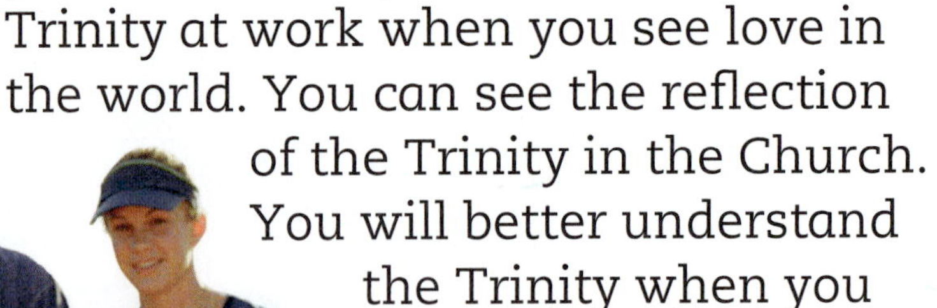

What other mystery of faith do you believe?

Chapter 5 The Church Worships

Let Us Pray

Leader: Holy Father, we celebrate your love for us.
"Give praise with tambourines and dance,
praise him with flutes and strings."
Psalm 150:4

All: Holy Father, we celebrate your love for us.
Amen.

Activity Let's Begin

Share the Joy The music was loud and lively. Each dancer moved separately, but the group moved together, too. Each dancer helped make the pattern of the dance.

Brendan and Maya imitated the way the dance leader moved. They were glad to be part of the dance. Together they shared the joy of the music and had a lot of fun.

- Act out a feeling by using dance or other body movements. Have classmates guess what you are feeling.

Explore

Stories of God's Love

Why do Church members celebrate together?

Catholics come together to celebrate the Mass. Parties or special meals are great ways to celebrate the joy of being part of God's community.

A STORY

The Joy of Celebrations

Kyle was not pleased. He felt far too hot, dressed in a suit and sitting in the car on the way to his grandparents' anniversary party.

"Mom," Kyle said, "why couldn't I have skipped the party and gone to practice?"

"We've been through this," said Kyle's mother. "This anniversary is a very special occasion, and you need to be part of it."

At the party Kyle was happy to see his cousins. There was good food and great music. Kyle especially enjoyed watching his grandparents dance.

On the way home, Kyle thought about how he acted on the way to the party. "Mom," he said, "I'm sorry I didn't want to go. When is the next family party?"

How does your family celebrate special occasions?

Celebrating Together

Jesus taught his followers how to celebrate. He told them stories and shared meals with them. His last meal with them was the most memorable one of all.

SCRIPTURE

Luke 22:14–20

The Last Supper

Jesus and his friends were together to celebrate the Jewish feast of Passover.

Jesus took some bread. He blessed it and broke it. He gave the bread to his friends, saying, "This is my body, which will be given for you; do this in memory of me."

Jesus then took the cup of wine and said, "This cup is the new covenant in my blood, which will be shed for you."

Based on *Luke 22:14–20*

Share Your Faith

Think: Imagine that you are at the Last Supper. What do you think Jesus means by his words?

Share: Talk about this with a group.

Act: Act out the story of the Last Supper with your classmates.

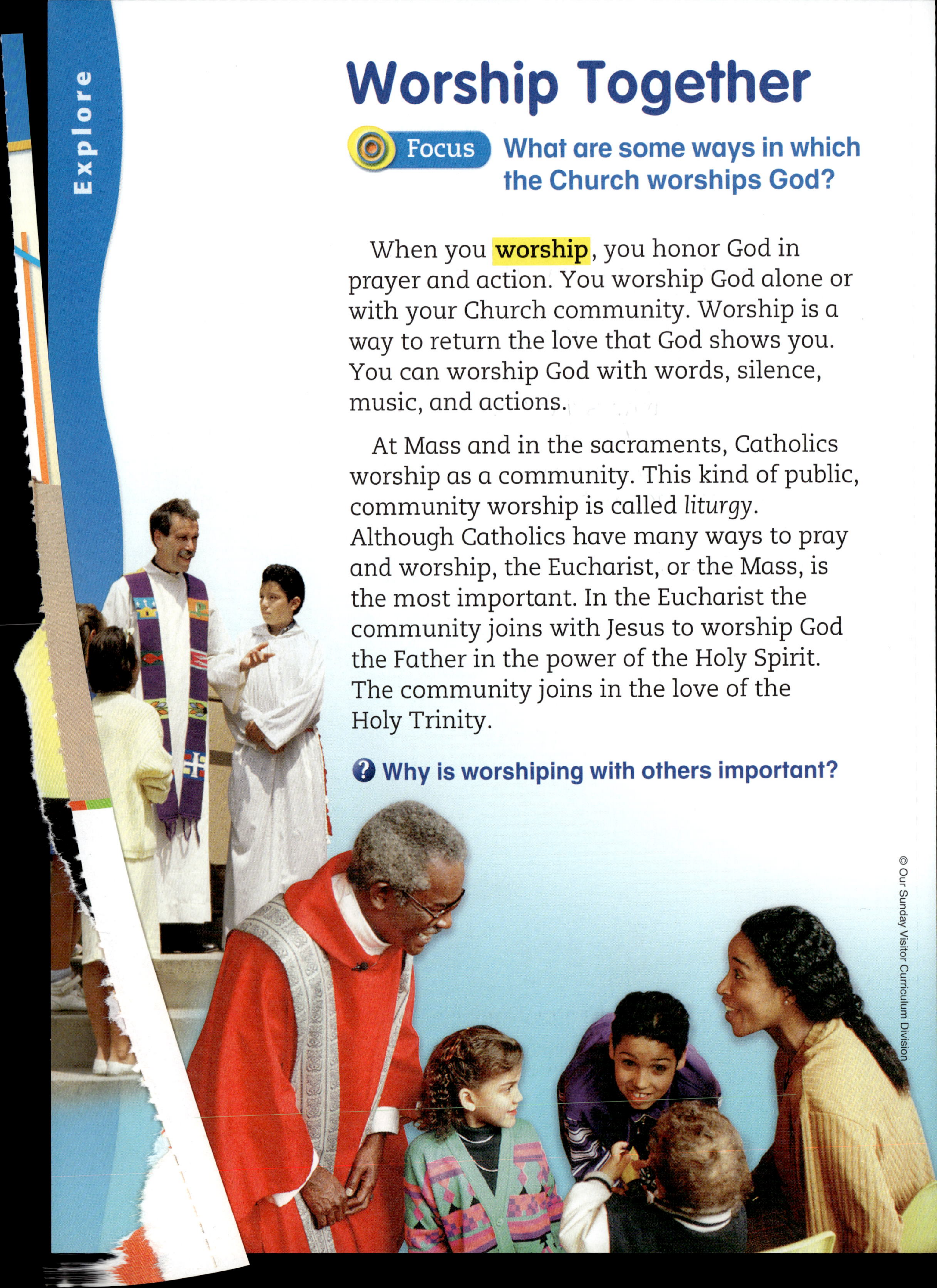

Worship Together

Focus **What are some ways in which the Church worships God?**

When you **worship**, you honor God in prayer and action. You worship God alone or with your Church community. Worship is a way to return the love that God shows you. You can worship God with words, silence, music, and actions.

At Mass and in the sacraments, Catholics worship as a community. This kind of public, community worship is called *liturgy*. Although Catholics have many ways to pray and worship, the Eucharist, or the Mass, is the most important. In the Eucharist the community joins with Jesus to worship God the Father in the power of the Holy Spirit. The community joins in the love of the Holy Trinity.

Why is worshiping with others important?

Center of the Church

At Mass, Catholics gather to hear God's word in Scripture. They also remember and celebrate what Jesus said and did with his disciples at the Last Supper. Every time you go to Mass, you are encouraged to receive Jesus' Body and Blood in Holy Communion. The Church requires that you do this at least once during the Easter Season.

The Church teaches that Catholics must attend Mass on Sundays and holy days because the Mass is the center of the Church's life. When you do this, you follow the third commandment, "Remember to keep holy the Lord's day."

Outside of Mass, Catholics also show love and respect for Jesus in the Eucharist by visiting the **Blessed Sacrament** in church. The blessed Bread from Mass, which has become the Body of Christ, is kept in the tabernacle. Jesus Christ is truly present in the Blessed Sacrament.

How does your family keep holy the Lord's day?

Words of Faith

To **worship** is to adore and honor God.

The **Blessed Sacrament** is the Holy Eucharist. This term especially refers to the blessed Bread that is kept in the tabernacle.

Activity

Give Praise Create a verse of joy, praise, or thanks for the gift of Eucharist. Say your words aloud, sing them, or dance them for your class. Write your verse in the space below.

____

____

Prayer of Praise

Gather and begin with the Sign of the Cross.

Sing together.

Glory to God. Glory to God.
Glory to God in the highest!
And on earth, peace on earth,
peace to people of good will.

All: Glory to God . . .

Reader: We praise you, we bless you,
we adore you, we glorify you,
we give you thanks for your great glory,
Lord God, heavenly King, O God, almighty Father.

All: Glory to God . . .

Reader: Lord Jesus Christ, Only Begotten Son,
Lord God, Lamb of God, Son of the Father,
you take away the sins of the world,
have mercy on us;
you take away the sins of the world,
receive our prayer;
you are seated at the right hand of the Father,
have mercy on us.

All: Glory to God . . .

Reader: For you alone are the Holy One,
you alone are the Lord,
you alone are the Most High,
Jesus Christ,
with the Holy Spirit
in the glory of God the Father.

All: Glory to God . . .

Chapter 6 Pray Always

Let Us Pray

Leader: O God, listen to our prayers.
"Hear my cry for help,
my king, my God!
To you I pray, O LORD."
Psalm 5:3

All: O God, listen to our prayers. Amen.

Activity Let's Begin

Hear Me, God Joel is praying to God. Imagine what God could be saying to answer him.

Joel: Lord, did you hear me singing at Mass on Sunday?

- What might God say to Joel?

Joel: Lord, sometimes it's hard to sing. I don't always know all the words.

- What advice might God give Joel?
- What do you say when you pray? Tell a partner.

Talking to God

What does Jesus teach you about prayer?

Jesus told this story about two people who talked to God.

SCRIPTURE Luke 18:9–14

The Pharisee and the Tax Collector

Two men went up to the temple to pray. One man, a Pharisee, walked proudly to the front of the temple. He looked at the other people and began his prayer.

"Dear God, I thank you that I am not like others. Other people want everything for themselves. They are not honest," he said.

"I know that I am better than that tax collector. I fast two times a week, and pay money to the temple," he said.

The tax collector stood at a distance. He looked down and prayed, "O God, be merciful to me a sinner."

Jesus told the people, "God was happy with the tax collector's prayer."

Based on *Luke 18:9–14*

Why was God happy with the tax collector's quiet prayer for forgiveness?

Jesus Teaches About Prayer

Jesus taught his followers that **prayer** is talking and listening to God. It is raising your mind and heart to God. When Jesus' followers asked him to teach them how to pray, he taught them the Lord's Prayer. Jesus told them to call upon God the Father, as he did. He also gave this advice.

Prayer is talking and listening to God. It is raising your mind and heart to God.

SCRIPTURE — Matthew 6:5–8

Praying Well

Jesus told his disciples not to be like the people who pray loudly in public so that others can see and hear them. To be seen is their reward. Jesus said that you should go to a private place, close the door, and pray quietly to the Father. God will hear you.

Some people think that God will hear them better if they use lots of fancy words to pray. Do not be like that. The Father knows what is in your heart even before you say it.

Based on *Matthew 6:5–8*

Where and for what do you pray most often?

Activity: Share Your Faith

Think: Do you have a quiet place in which to pray?

Share: Share your ideas for quiet "prayer places."

Act: Draw what your "prayer place" looks like.

Prayer Is Important

What are some different ways to pray?

Prayer was an important part of Jesus' life. Sometimes he got up early to pray. At other times he prayed all night. Jesus prayed for other people. He also prayed when he needed help.

Prayer should be an important part of your day, too. You can use your own words or prayers that you have memorized. You can even pray without words by just being quiet in the presence of God's love. But whenever you pray, you can be sure that many other Christians are praying at the very same time.

Where do you pray when you are at home?

Why Pray?

We pray for different reasons. To help you understand prayer better, here are five types, or forms, of prayer.

- **Blessing and adoration:** In a blessing prayer, you want to return the love and care God gives you. You adore God by worshiping him.
- **Praise:** You are amazed by God's greatness, and you pray to praise God.
- **Petition:** In times of need or when you sin, you ask God for help or forgiveness.
- **Intercession:** You ask for God's help for other people and for the whole community.
- **Thanksgiving:** You thank God for all the good things that he gives you.

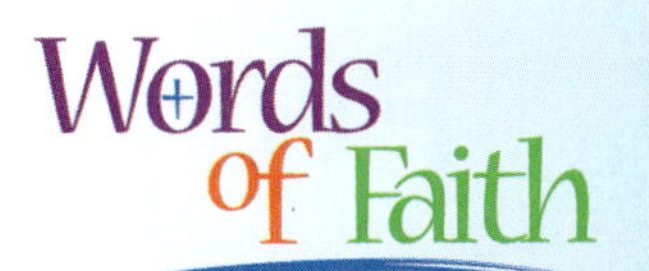

A prayer of **petition** is a request for something that you want or need.

Activity **Connect Your Faith**

Identify Prayers Work with a partner to find these Scripture verses. Tell which form of prayer each verse shows.

Psalm 51:3–5	Patition
Psalm 107:1	Thanksgiving
Psalm 125:4	intercession

BIBLE

Prayer of Petition

Gather and begin with the Sign of the Cross.

Sing together the refrain:

Our help comes from the Lord, the maker of heaven and earth.

Group 1: Help us remember to bless and adore you.

All: **Sing the refrain.**

Group 2: Help us remember to praise you, for you are wonderful.

All: **Sing the refrain.**

Group 1: Help us remember to turn to you whenever we need help.

All: **Sing the refrain.**

Group 2: Help us remember to ask you to help others who need you.

All: **Sing the refrain.**

Group 1: Help us remember to thank you, for you are so good to us.

All: **Sing the refrain.**

Leader: Let us pray.

Bow your heads as the leader prays.

All: Amen.

Review and Apply

A Work with Words Match each form of prayer in Column 1 with its definition in Column 2. Write the correct letter on the line provided.

	Column 1	Column 2
c	1. blessing	a. asking God to help other people
e	2. praise	b. telling God that you are grateful
d	3. petition	c. responding to God's love
a	4. intercession	d. asking God to help you
b	5. thanksgiving	e. recognizing God's greatness

B Check Understanding Tell one thing Jesus taught his followers about prayer.

You don't need fancy words

Activity Live Your Faith

Praying in Different Ways Imagine that someone who does not speak your language wants to learn to pray. What will you share with him or her without using words? Write your idea on the lines below.

I will:
fold my hands
and bow my head
and they will do it.

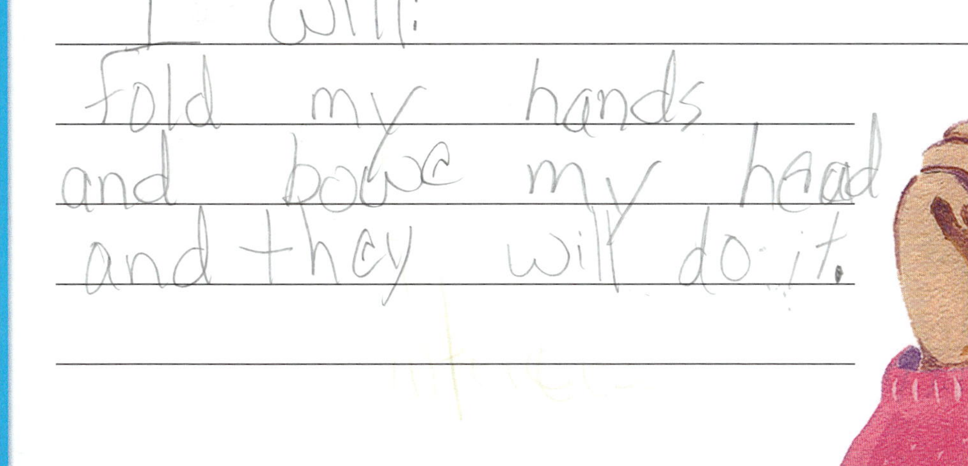

Family Faith

Catholics Believe

- Prayer is the raising of one's mind and heart to God.
- Prayer is an important part of a Christian's daily life.

SCRIPTURE

Matthew 6:9–13 is the Lord's Prayer, also called the Our Father. Pray the verses with your family. Talk about what the prayer means to you.

GO online **www.osvcurriculum.com**
For weekly scripture readings and seasonal resources

Activity
Live Your Faith

Say a Prayer As a family, write a letter to God. Use one of the five forms of prayer to tell God about your family's day or week. If you wish, light a candle and play reflective music. Have one family member prayerfully read the letter aloud.

People of Faith

▲ Thomas Merton 1915–1968

Thomas Merton was born in Paris, France and lived all over the world. One day, in Louisville, Kentucky, he realized that he felt connected to every person he saw. He decided to become a monk. He became a Catholic in 1938 and joined a Trappist monastery in Kentucky in 1941. Merton lived a simple life of prayer. He was a poet and wrote books about God.

Family Prayer

Almighty God, help us pray every moment of our lives and find you, as Thomas Merton did. Amen.

In Unit 2 your child is learning about the TRINITY.

CCC *See Catechism of the Catholic Church 2559, 2659 for further reading on chapter content.*

Unit 2 Review

A Work with Words Answer each question with the correct word from the Word Bank.

WORD BANK
blessing
praise
petition
intercession
thanksgiving

1. Which form of prayer asks God for forgiveness? ____________
2. Which form of prayer asks God to help other people? ____________
3. Which form of prayer thanks God for all the good things in your life? ____________
4. Which form of prayer recognizes God's greatness? ____________
5. Which form of prayer returns God's love? ____________

B Check Understanding Complete each sentence by circling the correct word.

6. The Holy Trinity is the (three/two) Persons in one God.
7. Catholics believe in the (questions/mysteries) of faith without completely understanding them.
8. The Church requires that you receive Holy Communion at least once each year during (Easter/Christmas) Season.
9. Catholics must attend (meetings/Mass) on Sundays and holy days.
10. The (rectory/tabernacle) holds the Holy Eucharist.

Unit 3
Jesus Christ

In this unit you will...

learn that Jesus came to tell people the good news of the kingdom of God. Jesus sacrificed his own life to save everyone from sin. By his life, death, Resurrection, and Ascension, Jesus gives all people the gift of new life with God that will last forever. The Church continues to spread Jesus' message of new life and hope.

What do you think you will learn in this unit about the Body of Christ?

Invite

Leader: Dear God, help us follow you always.

"You will show me the path to life,
abounding joy in your presence,
the delights at your right hand forever."

Psalm 16:11

All: Dear God, help us follow you always. Amen.

Activity Let's Begin

The Best News Ever Taleshia's religion book had these questions:

What's the best news you have ever heard?

"My dad got me a new kitten!" she wrote.

What did you do when you heard the news?

"I told all my friends," wrote Taleshia.

Why did you do that?

"I knew it would make them happy, too!"

- How do you share good news with others? Name three ways.

Sharing News

What good news does Jesus share?

Everyone wants to share good news. Jesus shared his good news through words and actions. Sometimes you share good news with pictures or through certain objects.

A STORY

Andrew's Kite

Andrew's friend, old Mr. Levy, lived by the park near Andrew's school. He always sat at his window and watched the kids playing.

One day Andrew stopped to talk to Mr. Levy. Mr. Levy said, "I have always liked rainbows. They remind me of God's love, but I hardly ever see rainbows."

Andrew thought of a rainbow kite in his closet. He got his friend Diego to help him.

The boys went to the park near Mr. Levy's house and flew the kite.

The next day, the boys saw Mr. Levy. He called out, "I got your message, boys. Thank you for sending me a rainbow!"

? What message did the boys send Mr. Levy with the rainbow kite?

Jesus Shares Good News

Andrew and Diego shared a happy message with Mr. Levy. The rainbow was a sign that they were thinking of him and wanted him to be happy. The good news Jesus shares is that God the Father loves his people and saves them from the power of sin and everlasting death.

Just as Jesus shares the good news of God's love with you, you pass it on to others. The work of the Catholic Church is to share the good news of Jesus in words and actions.

Another word for good news is *gospel*. The Church gives this name to the four books of the Bible that tell about Jesus' life and teachings. The **Gospels** are named for Matthew, Mark, Luke, and John. The Church reads from the Gospels at every Mass.

? How can you share Jesus' good news?

Words of Faith

The **Gospels** are the four books in the New Testament that tell the stories of Jesus' life, death, and Resurrection. They are the most important books for the Church because they focus on Jesus.

Activity Share Your Faith

Think: When have you spread the good news about Jesus?

Share: List words that would help describe the good news.

Act: Write a radio commercial that uses your words about the good news of Jesus, and read it to the class.

Explore

Jesus' Message

Focus What is the good news of God's kingdom?

Readings from the Bible, also called *Scripture*, are used every time the Church community gathers to worship. These readings were used to worship in Jesus' day, too.

SCRIPTURE Luke 4:16–22

Jesus in the Synagogue

One day, Jesus came back to his hometown of Nazareth. Everyone had gathered for worship. Jesus opened the Book of Isaiah and read words that described a person God promised to send.

"The Spirit of the Lord is upon me,
because He has anointed me
to bring glad tidings to the poor."

Jesus then said he had come to set people free and to make people who are blind see. He had come to announce a time of blessings from God.

Then Jesus surprised everyone. He said, "Today, this scripture passage has been fulfilled in your hearing."

Based on *Luke 4:16–22*

The people were surprised by Jesus' message. They were waiting for a **messiah**, or *savior*. They did not expect him to be a man from Nazareth.

Why were people surprised by Jesus' message?

God's Kingdom

The words Jesus read from Scripture tell about the **kingdom of God**, or the rule of justice and peace. In God's kingdom, those who are poor hear joyful news. No one is a prisoner of sin and sadness. People who are sick are healed.

Jesus told parables to describe the kingdom of God. For example, he said that the kingdom of God was like a mustard seed. This seed grows from a tiny seed into a large, beautiful tree. Jesus was planting the seed of the kingdom. Jesus showed people how to live. He healed people who were sick. He set people free from loneliness, sorrow, and sin. Jesus sends his Church to invite everyone into God's kingdom.

Words of Faith

Messiah is a Hebrew word that means *anointed*. Christians believe that Jesus is the Messiah—the one who has been anointed, or chosen.

The **kingdom of God** is God's rule of true justice, love, and peace.

How can you help the kingdom of God keep growing like the mustard seed?

Activity Connect Your Faith

Write a Headline Imagine yourself as a newspaper reporter in Nazareth on the day that Jesus read from the Book of Isaiah. What headline would you use for a story about this event in the local newspaper? Write it here.

Nazareth Times

Jesus reads the book of the bible.

Asking Prayer

Gather and begin with the Sign of the Cross.

Leader: Dear Jesus, you taught us in so many ways. You told us stories about God.

All: **Help us understand your lessons.**

Leader: You showed us how to act with kindness.

All: **Help us act as you did.**

Leader: You came to share your Father's love.

All: **Help us be more loving with our families and friends.**

Leader: You came to heal the sick and to forgive.

All: **Help us comfort those who are sick and lonely and forgive those who have hurt us.**

Leader: Let us pray.

Bow your heads as the leader prays.

All: **Amen.**

Sing together.

We are sent two by two.
Sent as church in the world.
Sent to share God's good
news, Sing and tell, spread
the Word.

CHAPTER 7

Review and Apply

Check Understanding Write or circle the correct responses.

1. The work of the Church is to ________________
________________________________.

2. Christians believe that Jesus is the ________________ who has been anointed, or chosen.

3. Jesus used ________________ to teach people something about God and his kingdom.

4. The word *gospel* means _____.
   a. storytelling
   b. good news
   c. religion

5. God's kingdom is _____.
   a. a country in the Middle East
   b. something that existed only in Bible times
   c. God's rule of peace and justice

Activity Live Your Faith

Spread Good News Design a bumper sticker that shares Jesus' message. Use the space below to combine words and art for your bumper sticker.

Family Faith

Catholics Believe

- Jesus shared the good news about God's kingdom of justice, love, and peace.
- Jesus is the Messiah, the chosen one and Savior.

SCRIPTURE

Read *Mark 8:27–30.* Talk about what these verses mean to you.

www.osvcurriculum.com
For weekly scripture readings and seasonal resources

Activity

Live Your Faith

Read the Bible Begin to share stories from the Bible at a regular time. Read together the parable of the farmer who planted good wheat seed. (See *Matthew 13:24–30.*) Talk about what this parable means. If you need help, read *Matthew 13:36–43.* You will find out how Jesus explained the parable.

▲ Saint Peter Canisius 1521–1597

People of Faith

Peter Canisius was born in Nijmegen, Germany, which is now part of the Netherlands. He found many ways to share God's good news. He taught people about the Catholic Church. Peter Canisius preached and celebrated the sacraments as he traveled. He is known for starting schools. Saint Peter Canisius's feast day is December 21.

Family Prayer

Saint Peter, pray for us that we may use our resources to share the word of God. Amen.

In Unit 3 your child is learning about the Jesus Christ.

CCC *See Catechism of the Catholic Church 546, 1154 for further reading on chapter content.*

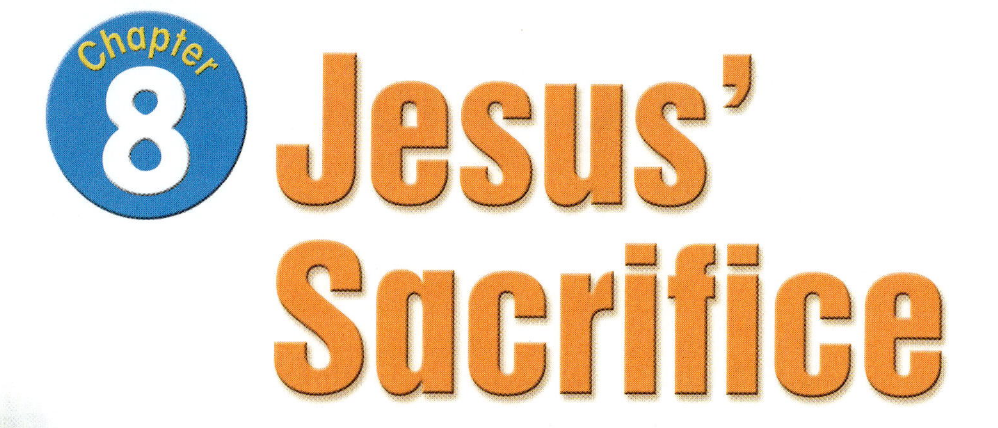

Chapter 8 Jesus' Sacrifice

Let Us Pray

Leader: Loving God, help us give of ourselves.

"Offer praise as your sacrifice to
God;
fulfill your vows to the Most High."

Psalm 50:14

All: Loving God, help us give of ourselves. Amen.

Activity Let's Begin

Change

Selfish
stingy, greedy
grab, take, want
thoughtless, uncaring, loving, kind
share, help, give
generous, endless
Selfless

This diamante poem shows a change from selfish to selfless. Like the poem, people can change from being selfish to being selfless, too.

- How do you turn a selfish act into one of kindness?

Making Choices

What does it mean to make a sacrifice?

Jesus made a promise to his Father. A promise can be easy or difficult to keep. You may need to give something up to keep a promise. Read this story about keeping promises.

A STORY

Gina's Promise

One day Gina was faced with a difficult choice. She was having fun with her friends when suddenly she stopped and looked at her watch.

"It's late. I have to go," Gina said.

"Call and say you're playing," Martina said.

"I made a promise. I have to go," Gina said.

At the care center, Aunt Margaret smiled brightly. "Hello, Gina. I am so glad to see you!"

"I promised to go for a walk with you."

Aunt Margaret smiled and said, "Great! Let's go!"

What did Gina give up?

Sacrifices Show Love

Gina gave up an afternoon with friends because she made a promise. When you give up something or do something difficult out of love, it is called a **sacrifice**. It is not easy to make a sacrifice. It takes a lot of love and courage. You have to be unselfish when you make a sacrifice.

Jesus' Sacrifice

Jesus chose to make the greatest sacrifice of all. He did something that no one else could do. Jesus gave up his life so that people could be saved from the power of sin and everlasting death. He freely gave up his life so that all people could have new life with God forever.

When have you made a sacrifice for someone? How do sacrifices show love?

Words of Faith

To **sacrifice** is to give up something for a greater good.

Activity: Share Your Faith

Think: Would you give up playtime with your friends to help a family member?

Share: Talk to your group about a time when you made a sacrifice.

Act: Write about how this sacrifice made you feel.

____

____

____

Jesus' Resurrection

What does the Paschal mystery mean?

Jesus' loving choice fulfilled God's plan to save his people. Through the work of the Holy Spirit, the Father raised Jesus from death to new life. This is called the **Resurrection**. The Resurrection showed that God's power is stronger than death.

SCRIPTURE John 20:11–18

Mary Meets Jesus

Mary Magdalene went to Jesus' tomb, but she found it empty. She thought that people had taken Jesus' body away. Then angels spoke to her, and she heard someone call her name. When she turned, Jesus was there!

When Mary first saw Jesus, she didn't recognize him. Thinking that he was the gardener, she asked where Jesus was. He said, "Mary!"

Then she knew who Jesus was. She called him *Teacher*. He told her to tell his friends that he was returning to the Father.

Based on *John 20:11–18*

How is the news of Jesus' Resurrection shared today?

The Paschal Mystery

Jesus' suffering, death, Resurrection, and Ascension are called the **Paschal mystery**. The word *Paschal* comes from a word that means "passover." Jesus died to save people from their sins at the time of year when Jews celebrate Passover. Jesus was raised from the dead and ascended into heaven. He "passed over" from death to life so that all people can have new life with God in heaven.

The Mass and the sacraments are ways that the Church lives out this great mystery. When you take part in the celebration of the Eucharist, you share in the saving power of the Paschal mystery.

Words of Faith

The **Resurrection** is the event of Jesus' being raised from death to new life by God the Father through the power of the Holy Spirit.

The **Paschal mystery** is the mystery of Jesus' suffering, death, Resurrection, and Ascension.

Activity Connect Your Faith

Create a Crucifix Jesus' suffering, death, Resurrection, and Ascension can give you hope during hard or sad times. Draw a picture of a crucifix, or create one from clay, wood, or some other material. Look at it during difficult times, and remember Jesus' saving actions.

Celebrate

Prayer of Praise

Gather and begin with the Sign of the Cross.

Sing together the refrain.

Sing a new song. Sing of Christ who rose from the dead.

Alleluia! Alleluia! Sing a new song.

Leader: We gather to praise God.
We are grateful to him for the sacrifice of his Son, Jesus. The mystery of faith:

All: **We proclaim your Death, O Lord, and profess your Resurrection until you come again.**

Sing the refrain.

Leader: Let us pray.

Bow your heads as the leader prays.

All: **Amen.**

Review and Apply

Check Understanding Write or circle the correct response.

1. A ____________________ is giving up something for a greater good.
2. Jesus ____________________ to save people from the power of sin and everlasting death.
3. ____________________ shared with the Apostles the news of Jesus' Resurrection.
4. The suffering, death, Resurrection, and Ascension of Jesus are called the _____.
   - **a.** mystery of the Trinity
   - **b.** Paschal mystery
   - **c.** Sign of the Cross
5. You share in the mystery of Jesus' suffering, death, Resurrection, and Ascension when you _____.
   - **a.** take part in the celebration of the Eucharist
   - **b.** decorate the Christmas tree
   - **c.** look at a sunrise

Activity Live Your Faith

Remember a Sacrifice Write a thank-you note to someone who has made a sacrifice for you.

____

____

____

____

Thank You

Family Faith

Catholics Believe

- Jesus died and rose to new life to save all people from the power of sin.
- The Church celebrates the Paschal mystery in all of the sacraments.

SCRIPTURE

Mark 15:33–41 is about Jesus' death. Read this story and talk with your family about its meaning.

GO online **www.osvcurriculum.com** For weekly scripture readings and seasonal resources

Activity

Live Your Faith

Give Thanks Your family is a school of faith. You learn the meaning of sacrifice at home as others sacrifice for you and you sacrifice for them. Share a special meal together. At the meal, take turns thanking each member of the family for a sacrifice that he or she has made for the family.

▲ Saint Mary Magdalene first century A.D.

People of Faith

Mary Magdalene was a follower of Jesus. She stood at the foot of Jesus' cross as he suffered and died. She went to Jesus' tomb on the first Easter morning. She was the first to tell others about Jesus' Resurrection. Her feast day is July 22.

Family Prayer

Saint Mary, pray for us that we may appreciate Jesus' sacrifice and feel the joy of his Resurrection. Amen.

In Unit 3 your child is learning about the JESUS CHRIST.

CCC *See Catechism of the Catholic Church 613, 1085 for further reading on chapter content.*

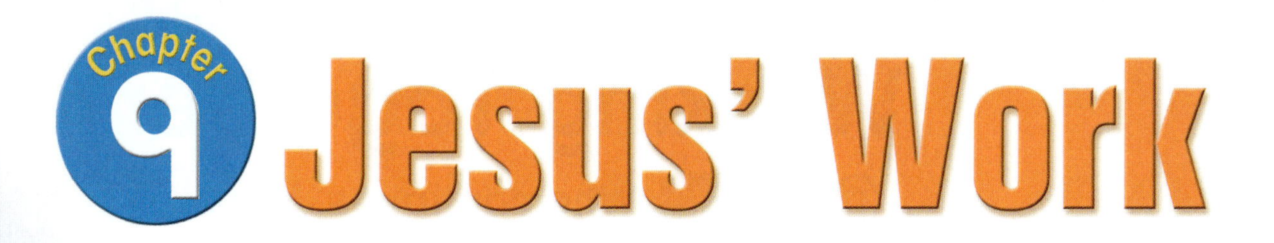

Chapter 9 Jesus' Work

Let Us Pray

Leader: Loving God, bring hope and comfort to all people.

"Defend the lowly and fatherless;
render justice to the afflicted and needy."

Psalm 82:3

All: Loving God, bring hope and comfort to all people. Amen.

Activity Let's Begin

A Big Success The class play took a lot of work. It was a big success because everyone helped. "Let's do this again!" the children all agreed. "We work well together."

- Describe a situation in which you worked well with others. What happened?

Working Together

Who continues Jesus' work today?

When people work together, the job is easier for everyone. This story tells how important working together can be.

A STORY

Kerry's Friends

"What's wrong?" asked Kerry when she saw her sister Erin crying at the table.

"I offered to help the church office send out these letters, but I am running out of time. They need to go in the mail today, and I still have fifty more to do," cried Erin.

"Don't worry, I'll find help," replied Kerry.

Soon, Kerry's friends came to help. Curtis stuffed the envelopes and Felicia sealed them. Kerry and Rachel put on the stamps. Then Erin and her mom rushed the letters to the post office.

"Thank you so much for your help," said Erin when she returned home. "It's amazing how quickly a job can be completed when everyone works together."

When have you worked with others to help solve a problem?

The Church

Like the children in the story, the people of the Church work together. When Jesus lived on earth, he did his Father's work. The Holy Spirit was with Jesus. At his Ascension, Jesus returned to his Father in heaven. Then Jesus sent the Spirit to be with his Church. The Holy Spirit makes it possible for the Church to continue Jesus' work today.

As a baptized member of the Church family, you are Jesus to other people. You use your hands and feet, your mouth and ears, and your mind and heart to do Jesus' work. One name for the Church is the **Body of Christ**. This name tells you that all Church members are one, as the parts of a body are one. It also says that you belong to Jesus.

Why is the Body of Christ a good name for the Church?

Words of Faith

The **Body of Christ** is a name for the Church, of which Christ is the head. All of the baptized are members of the Body of Christ.

Share Your Faith

Think: When is the Church a community that helps others?

Share: With a group, write a short song about working together to help others.

Act: Sing your song to the class.

Doing Jesus' Work

Focus How does the Church do Jesus' work?

Catholics become members of the Body of Christ at Baptism.

The Church continues to do Jesus' work on earth. But what exactly should Jesus' followers do? Jesus explained how to care for people who need help. He said that people who loved God and others were doing his work. Jesus told his followers this story. In it, Jesus speaks of himself as a king.

SCRIPTURE Matthew 25:34–40

Those Who Helped

At the end of time, the king will call all people before him. To some people, the king will say, "Enter into the kingdom and be joyful! When I was hungry, you fed me. You gave me water when I was thirsty and clothes when I needed them. When I was in prison, you visited me."

The people will say, "When did we do these things for you?"

The king will say, "Whenever you helped anyone in need, you helped me."

Based on *Matthew 25:34–40*

How can you help Jesus by helping someone else?

Share Your Gifts

God gave each person special gifts, or *talents*. A talent is something you enjoy doing and can do well. You are called to use your talents to serve others. The Church is one, but it has many kinds of members with many kinds of gifts.

Everyone has different talents. When people put their talents together and work as the Body of Christ, they can do more than any one person can do alone.

At the end of Mass, you go forth to do Jesus' work in the world. The priest or deacon says, "Go in peace, glorifying the Lord by your life." You glorify the Lord by loving and serving all of God's people.

? How many different talents can you count among the people in your classroom?

Activity Connect Your Faith

Share Your Talents Design a banner that shows what some of your talents are and how you can use them to help others.

Asking Prayer

Gather and begin with the Sign of the Cross.

Leader: God our Father, we stand before you as the Body of Christ.

Reader 1: Help our eyes see work that needs to be done,

All: **So that we can help one another.**

Reader 2: Help our ears hear those who ask for help,

All: **So that we can help one another.**

Reader 1: Help our hands and feet be strong,

All: **So that we can help one another.**

Reader 2: Help our hearts be full of love,

All: **So that we can help one another.**

Leader: Let us pray.

Bow your heads as the leader prays.

All: **Amen.**

Sing together.

We are many parts, we are all one body,
and the gifts we have we are given to share.
May the Spirit of love make us one indeed;
one, the love we share, one, our hope in
despair, one, the cross that we bear.

CHAPTER 9

Review and Apply

Check Understanding Write or circle the correct answer.

1. The Church is sometimes called _____ because it is made up of many members who work together in Jesus' name.
   a. heaven on earth
   b. the keeper of the keys
   c. the Body of Christ
2. How do you glorify the Lord?

   ____

   ____

3. Since Jesus returned to his Father, who does Jesus' work on earth?

   ____

4. When Jesus returned to heaven, whom did he send to be with the Church?

   ____

5. Name three ways you can continue Jesus' work by helping others.

   ____

   ____

Activity Live Your Faith

Use Your Talents Design a poster to encourage people to use their talents to help one another as members of the Body of Christ. If possible, enlarge your design, and put it on poster board to display it.

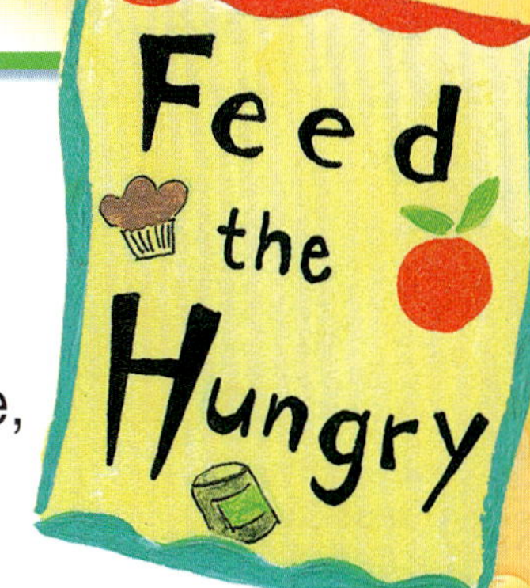

Family Faith

Catholics Believe

- The Church is the Body of Christ, to which all members belong.
- Church members continue Jesus' work when they help others.

SCRIPTURE

John 15:1–5, 7–10 is about being a member of the Body of Christ. Talk about how your family is part of the Body of Christ.

www.osvcurriculum.com
For weekly scripture readings and seasonal resources

Activity

Live Your Faith

Share Your Talents As members of the Body of Christ, decide how your unique combination of talents could be used in a project to help someone in need. Do the project with your family, or join with others who may have useful talents.

People of Faith

▲ Saint Mary Ann of Quito 1618–1645

Mary Ann was born in Quito, a city in Ecuador, South America. She was from a noble family. At an early age, she promised to live a holy life in poverty. She spent much time in prayer and acts of penance. She left home only to attend Mass. She gave food to people and taught children in her home. She was blessed with the gift of healing. Saint Mary Ann's feast day is May 26.

Family Prayer

Saint Mary Ann, pray for us that we may serve God by serving those who ask us for help. Amen.

In Unit 3 your child is learning about the Jesus Christ.

CCC *See Catechism of the Catholic Church 521, 1267 for further reading on chapter content.*

Unit 3 Review

A Work with Words Match each description in Column 1 with the correct term in Column 2.

Column 1

_____ 1. Teaching stories that Jesus told

_____ 2. Jesus made a great _____ for us.

_____ 3. A name for the Church, of which Christ is the head

_____ 4. A Hebrew word that means "anointed"

_____ 5. Jesus' suffering, death, Resurrection, and Ascension

Column 2

a. Messiah

b. Paschal mystery

c. parables

d. Body of Christ

e. sacrifice

B Check Understanding Circle the letter of the choice that best completes the sentence or answers the question.

6. The four books about Jesus in the New Testament are the _____.
   a. parables b. Gospels c. Bibles

7. The kingdom of God is also called God's _____.
   a. reign b. promise c. justice

8. What happened three days after Jesus' death?
   a. Visitation b. Resurrection c. Ascension

9. The Gospels are named for Matthew, Mark, Luke, and _____.
   a. James b. Joseph c. John

10. Whom did Jesus send to us after he returned to heaven?
    a. Holy Spirit b. Apostles c. Mary

Unit 4 The Church

In this unit you will...

learn that the Church is <u>one</u> because she is united in the unity of the Trinity, and she has one founder, Jesus. The Church's soul is the Holy Spirit, who brings together her members. The Church is holy because she is united to Christ who is holy. The Church is catholic, or universal, because she has all the truths and means of salvation. Her work is to share Jesus' message with the whole world. The Church is apostolic because she was founded by Jesus, on Peter and the Apostles. The Pope and bishops, as successors of the Apostles, lead the Church.

What do you think you will learn in this unit about the Catholic Church?

Chapter 10

Church Leaders

Let Us Pray

Leader: Caring God, help us follow your will for our lives.

"With your counsel you guide me,
and at the end receive me with
honor."

Psalm 73:24

All: Caring God, help us follow your will for our lives. Amen.

Activity Let's Begin

Everyone Needs Leaders

Leaders help people know what to do. Good leaders know how to teach and guide. They know what needs to be done. They can figure out how to get each person to do the best job possible. It takes a special person to be a good leader.

- What kind of leader do you hope to be? When and how are you a leader now?

Explore

The First Leader

What did Jesus choose Peter to do for his Church?

Here is a story about the first leader of the Catholic Church.

SCRIPTURE Matthew 16:15–19, 26:69–75; John 21:15–17

Peter and Jesus

SCENE 1

Jesus: Who do you say that I am?

Simon: You are the Christ, the Son of God.

Jesus: Simon, no human told you to say that. God told you to say that. Your name is now Peter.

Narrator: *Peter* means "rock."

Jesus: Upon you, Peter, I will build my church. I will give you the keys to the kingdom of heaven. Evil will never overpower you.

SCENE 2

Narrator: On the night Jesus was betrayed, Peter followed him to the high priest's house.

Servant 1: You were with Jesus tonight, weren't you?

Peter: No, no, I don't know him.

Servant 2: This man was with Jesus.

Peter: No, I don't even know who Jesus is!

Servant 3: I saw you with him!

Peter: No! I don't know Jesus!

[Sound of a rooster crowing.]

Narrator: Peter remembers. Jesus said that Peter would deny him three times before the rooster crowed.

Peter: What have I done? [Cries.]

SCENE 3

Narrator: After his Resurrection, Jesus showed himself to his followers.

Jesus: Simon Peter, do you love me?

Peter: Jesus, you know that I love you.

Jesus: Feed my lambs. Do you love me?

Peter: Yes, you know that I love you.

Jesus: Take care of my sheep. Do you love me?

Peter: You must know that I love you.

Jesus: Feed my sheep.

Based on *Matthew 16:15–19, Matthew 26:69–75, John 21:15–17*

? Why do you think Jesus asked Peter the same question three times?

Activity Share Your Faith

Think: Have you ever been asked to be a leader?

Share: Talk about your experience in leading a group to which you belong. Was leading easy or difficult?

Act: Take turns leading your class in prayer or song.

Explore

Lead and Serve

Focus **How do the pope and bishops lead the Church?**

The **Apostles** were chosen by Jesus to be the first leaders of the Church. They carried out Jesus' mission of preaching the good news and saving people. Jesus chose Peter to be the leader of the Apostles.

Peter became the head of the Church on earth because Jesus chose Peter to be the first leader of the Apostles. The person in this position is now called the *pope*. The pope is in charge of caring for all of God's people. The word *pope* comes from an Italian word that means "father."

The pope is also the Bishop of Rome. The word *bishop* means "overseer." The **bishops** lead the whole Church. Each bishop leads and serves a diocese. The pope and bishops carry on the work of the Apostles in leading, guiding, and caring for God's people.

The Apostles' teaching and authority have been handed down to the bishops, who are the leaders of the Church today. They are the people who now take the place of the Apostles on earth.

What do you think the responsibilities of a bishop are?

Faith Fact

Bishops must travel to Rome every three to ten years to meet with the pope.

Leaders of the Parish

Dioceses are made up of many parishes. Each parish has leaders, too. The pastor is a priest who has been given the authority to lead a parish community. He celebrates the sacraments and works with others to serve the people of the parish. Deacons are ordained to celebrate some of the sacraments and to do works of charity.

The **Apostles** were the first twelve leaders called by Jesus.

Bishops are ordained to work with the pope in teaching and guiding the Church. They are the successors of the Apostles.

Church Members Serve

There are other people in a parish who are called to serve and lead. These men and women are not ordained, but they help with many parish ministries. Your catechist is one of these people. Other examples include liturgical ministers, parish committee members, and directors of religious education and youth ministry.

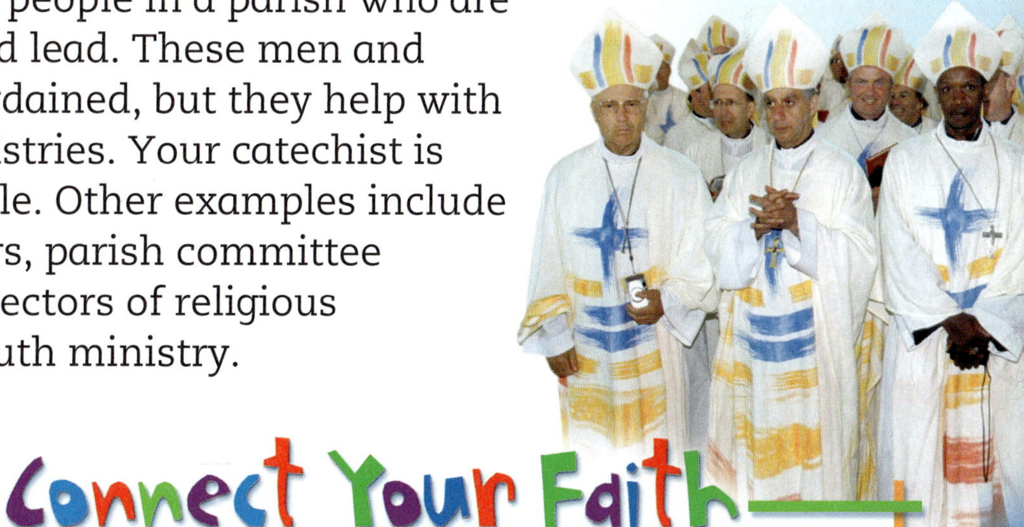

Activity Connect Your Faith

My Church Community Fill in the blanks to show how you belong to the community of the Church.

My name is Amanda.

I belong to holy family parish in the (Arch)diocese of clevlend.

Our pastor is Fater posing.

Our (arch)bishop is lenene.

Pope Frances and the bishops lead the Catholic Church.

Asking Prayer

Gather and begin with the Sign of the Cross.

Leader: We gather today to pray for our leaders and for the needs of the Church.

Reader 1: For the pope, the bishops, the priests, and other Church leaders, that they may act with wisdom and justice, we pray to the Lord.

All: **Lord, hear our prayer.**

Reader 2: For our teachers and catechists, that they may help us understand your plan for us, we pray to the Lord.

All: **Lord, hear our prayer.**

Reader 3: For all members of the Church, that we may use our gifts to serve, we pray to the Lord.

All: **Lord, hear our prayer.**

Leader: Let us pray.

Bow your heads as the leader prays.

All: **Amen.**

Sing together.

God ever faithful,
God ever merciful,
God of your people,
hear our prayer.

Review and Apply

Work with Words Match each description in Column 1 with the correct term in Column 2.

Column 1

 **1.** leads the whole Church on earth

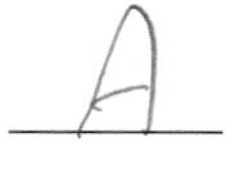 **2.** chose the Apostles to lead the Church

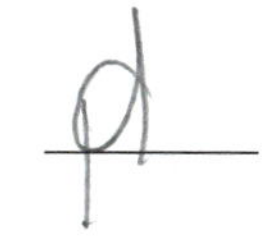 **3.** was the first leader of the Apostles

 **4.** leads a diocese

 **5.** leads a parish

Column 2

a. Jesus

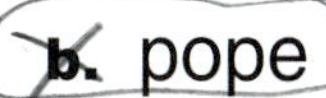

b. pope

c. bishop

d. Peter

e. pastor

Activity Live Your Faith

Think About Leadership Write a description of what a bishop, priest, deacon, or parish catechist does. List three good qualities that such a person needs in his or her work.

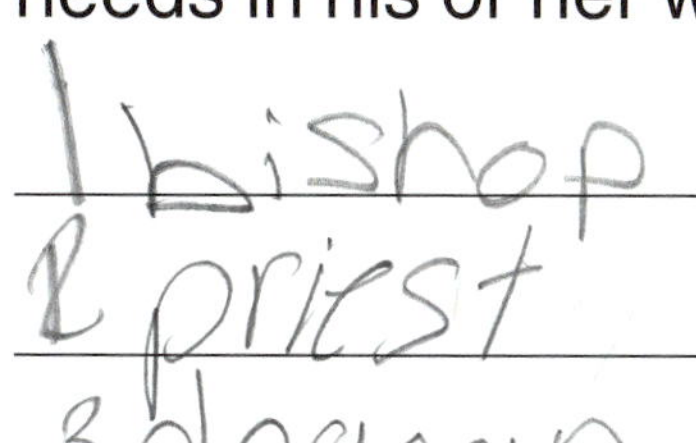

Family Faith

Catholics Believe

- The bishops are the successors of the Apostles.
- The pope, bishops, and pastors lead and guide the Church.

SCRIPTURE

1 Corinthians 3:10–11 is about building a foundation. Talk about how you can build up the Church.

www.osvcurriculum.com
For weekly scripture readings and seasonal resources

Activity
Live Your Faith

Do Research Bishops write letters to all the faithful of their dioceses from time to time. These letters guide the people on matters of faith. Find out about the last letter your bishop wrote to the people of your diocese. You can probably find the letter on the Web site for your diocese, or your pastor can help you find it.

People of Faith

▲ Saint Gregory the Great
c. 540–604

Gregory was born in Rome. He sold what he owned to help the poor. After he became pope, he trained missionaries, who traveled to England and worked to free slaves and preach the Gospel. Gregory's writings helped people learn about God. Music called Gregorian chant is named for him. Saint Gregory's feast day is September 3.

Family Prayer

Saint Gregory, pray for us that we may use our talents to serve others. Amen.

In Unit 4 your child is learning about the CHURCH.

CCC *See Catechism of the Catholic Church 816, 939 for further reading on chapter content.*

Invite

Chapter 11 One Holy People

Let Us Pray

Leader: Lord God, help us do your work.
"Unless the LORD build the house,
they labor in vain who build."
Psalm 127:1

All: Lord God, help us do your work. Amen.

Activity Let's Begin

One from Many

One tiny thread and then another
Woven tightly into place.
Six more threads, another color
Build the pattern, shape the space.
When Weaver Woman's work is done
There is a whole where once was none.

- Which is stronger, a single thread or a whole piece of cloth? Why?

Explore

Together in the Church

How is the Catholic Church one?

This letter explores how Church communities are sometimes different, but all are one in Jesus.

A STORY

Jackie's Visit

Dear Mom,

I'm having fun visiting Uncle Mike and Aunt Theresa. Yesterday we went to their parish church. The building was round! I could look past the altar and see people facing me! There were people of all different colors.

Then Mass started and I felt right at home. The priest was praying words I knew. There were scripture readings, just like at home. The songbook was different, but I knew the songs.

I can see that what makes our Church is what people believe and how they honor God.

Love,
Jackie

? How is your church the same as the one Jackie visited? How is it different?

Around the World

In other cultures, you would see some differences in the Mass celebration.

- In Africa, children might dance up the aisle in procession to the rhythm of drums.
- In India, the deacon might honor the Book of the Gospels by passing a tray of fragrant flowers over it.
- In many other countries, the language and music of the liturgy would be different.

The same mystery of faith is being celebrated in all these places. Christ is present, uniting the people. The main parts of the Mass are the same everywhere because the Catholic Church is one.

Activity: Share Your Faith

Think: How do you think Mass is celebrated in different parts of the world?

Share: Using a map or a globe, choose a country. Discuss with your group how Mass in that country might be different from Mass in the United States.

Act: Draw a picture of how Mass might look in the country you chose.

One Church

What makes the Catholic Church holy?

People from many different countries were united when the Holy Spirit came to followers of Jesus on **Pentecost**. Pentecost is the beginning of the Church. From that day on, the people understood more clearly that they were one body of believers who had been made holy.

SCRIPTURE — Acts 2:1–12

The Feast of Pentecost

Fifty days after Jesus was raised from the dead, his followers were together in a house in Jerusalem. Suddenly the house was filled with a noise like wind. Tongues of fire came to rest on each person in the room. All were filled with the Holy Spirit. They began speaking languages that they did not know.

Jerusalem was filled with Jews from all over the world that day. They heard the Apostles preaching. They were amazed that they could understand people from Galilee in their own languages.

Based on *Acts 2:1–12*

What happened after the Holy Spirit came to the Apostles at Pentecost?

United in Faith

The Holy Spirit continues to unify the Church today and make it holy. The Spirit guides the leaders of the Church. The Spirit guides you to follow Jesus more closely.

Catholics all over the world are united by their faith in Christ. The Church is even united with the saints, holy people of faith who are with God in heaven. The Church honors the saints, especially Mary, the Mother of Jesus, for their holiness. Christians can learn from the examples of the saints.

The Church is sometimes called the **communion of saints**. This means that the members of the Church on earth, in purgatory, and in heaven are all united. The saints join you in worshiping the Father, the Son, and the Holy Spirit.

Whom do you know who belongs to the communion of saints?

Words of Faith

Pentecost celebrates the coming of the Holy Spirit fifty days after Easter.

The **communion of saints** is made up of everyone who has been redeemed by Jesus—people on earth, people who have died and are in purgatory, and the saints in heaven.

Connect Your Faith

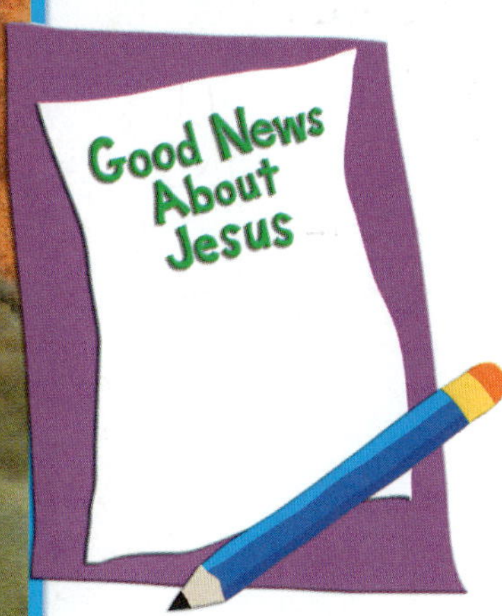

Tell the Good News The Holy Spirit made the disciples brave enough to share the good news of Jesus. Write some good news of Jesus that you think they may have shared. Tell your class.

____

____

Prayer of Petition

Gather and begin with the Sign of the Cross.

Leader: Come, Holy Spirit, fill the hearts of your faithful.

All: **And kindle in them the fire of your love.**

Leader: Send forth your Spirit and they shall be created.

All: **And you will renew the face of the earth.**

Leader: Lord, by the light of the Holy Spirit you have taught the hearts of your faithful. In the same Spirit, help us choose what is right and always rejoice in your consolation.

All: **Through Christ our Lord. Amen.**

Leader: Let us pray.

Bow your heads as the leader prays.

All: **Amen.**

Sing together.

Veni Sancte Spiritus;
Veni Sancte Spiritus;
Veni, veni, Sancte Spiritus;
Veni Sancte Spiritus.

"Veni Sancte Spiritus (Come Holy Spirit)"
© 1981, 1982, Christopher Walker.

Review and Apply

Check Understanding Circle True if a statement is true, and circle False if a statement is false. Correct any false statements.

1. The Holy Spirit unifies the Church today.

   True False ______________________________

2. Saints are holy people of faith.

   True False ______________________________

3. The Church is called the communion of saints because only saints can receive Communion.

   True False ______________________________

4. The communion of saints is made up entirely of people who have died.

   True False ______________________________

5. Pentecost is celebrated fifty days after Easter.

   True False ______________________________

Activity Live Your Faith

Design a Banner Use words and actions that describe the Holy Spirit. Think first of what the Holy Spirit does.

Words	Actions
____________________	____________________
____________________	____________________
____________________	____________________

CHAPTER 11

Family Faith

Catholics Believe

- The Holy Spirit unites the Church and makes it holy.
- Many cultures together make up the unity of the Church.

SCRIPTURE

John 20:21–23 tells of Jesus' gift of the Holy Spirit to guide his followers on earth.

www.osvcurriculum.com
For weekly scripture readings and seasonal resources

Activity

Live Your Faith

Holy at Home The family is the church of the home. That means that you are called to be one and holy. Discuss the best way that your family shows unity and one thing that would make your family a stronger unit. Ask the Holy Spirit to help you. The Spirit is the source of your holiness.

▲ Saints Perpetua and Felicity died c. A.D. 202–203

People of Faith

Perpetua and **Felicity** died together for their faith in northern Africa. Perpetua was a noblewoman who became a Christian. She kept a journal recording what happened to her in prison because of her faith. Felicity was a slave and a Christian. Both women were young mothers. They helped and comforted each other during their time in prison. Their feast day is March 7.

Family Prayer

Saints Perpetua and Felicity, pray for us and show us how to unite with other believers into a holy Church. Amen.

In Unit 4 your child is learning about the CHURCH.

CCC *See Catechism of the Catholic Church 813, 814 for further reading on chapter content.*

Chapter 12 The Church's Mission

Let Us Pray

Leader: Jesus, help us share your message.
"Yet their report goes forth through
all the earth,
their message, to the ends of
the world."

Psalm 19:5

All: Jesus, help us share your message. Amen.

Activity Let's Begin

On a Mission A mission is a particular job or duty that someone undertakes.

Once there was a farm boy who set off on a mission to find a treasure. The farm boy had to pass through a dangerous forest along the way, but a brave elf offered to help.

- What happens next in the story? Think of an ending to complete the story.

Explore

Planting the Seeds

Focus **What seeds do Christians plant?**

The opening story was about someone on a mission. Here is another story about a man who discovered his true mission.

A STORY

Johnny's Job

"Who's asleep under our apple tree?"

"Don't wake him," said Willie's mom.

The old man's eyes opened. He said, "I love to see apple blossoms. They remind me that good things are coming soon."

"You're Johnny Appleseed. You planted apple seeds everywhere! Dad said you planted some here."

"Yes. I've traveled and planted for over thirty years. I planted these trees long ago. They must give lots of apples!"

"They do. Would you like some?" Willie asked.

"I would love some. That's why I plant trees—so no one will be hungry."

? How does this story remind you of Jesus' teachings?

Sharing God's Good News

Johnny Appleseed traveled on a mission to share the good things of the earth. The Apostle Paul traveled on a mission to start new Christian communities. He wrote letters back to these communities, continuing to share the good news about God.

SCRIPTURE I Corinthians 3:5–9

Doing God's Work

Who is Paul? Who is Apollos? We are ministers through whom you became believers. I planted the seed. My helper Apollos watered the seed. Then God made the seed grow. The planter and the waterer are not nearly as important as God is, because it is God who makes things grow. Apollos and I are God's coworkers. You are God's field.

Based on *I Corinthians 3:5–9*

What was the seed that the Apostle Paul planted?

Activity Share Your Faith

Think: Remember some of the good works you have done to make the Church stronger.

Share: In a small group, tell about some of these works.

Act: Draw an apple tree on a separate sheet of paper. Add a new apple each time you do a good work.

The Church Is Catholic

How does the Church fulfill its mission?

Paul helped the early Christians know that the Church was for everyone. The Church is catholic because it is for all people in all times and places. The word *catholic* means "universal" or "everywhere."

The Church is apostolic because Jesus gave his Apostles the **mission** of sharing his good news with people all over the world.

The word *mission* also means a church community in another country or in a remote place where people need to hear the word of God. The term is sometimes used to describe a church with few members.

Missionaries are people who travel to share Jesus' good news, just as Paul did. You can help the Church's missionaries by praying for them and the people with whom they work. You can write letters to them and help raise money for things that the missionaries need.

What can Catholics do to continue the Church's mission?

Sharing with Others

Along with spreading the good news of Jesus, missionaries also share food, shelter, medical supplies, and other things with the people who need their help. These things are important because they provide for people's basic needs. Christians have always shared with others and been concerned for their needs.

God wants you to share not only physical things, such as food, but also spiritual, or holy, things. That is why Christian missionaries teach the people about Jesus and build churches, hospitals, and schools. They want to be sure that people everywhere hear God's good news.

How can you share the good news with other people?

Words of Faith

A **mission** is a job or duty that someone takes responsibility for. The Church's mission is to announce the good news of God's kingdom.

Missionaries are people who travel to share Jesus' good news.

Activity Connect Your Faith

Do God's Work Find out who in your parish or diocese is serving God as a missionary in another country or in a faraway place in this country. On a separate sheet of paper, design a card for him or her and add a note of thanks.

Asking Prayer

Gather and begin with the Sign of the Cross.

Leader: Dear Jesus, help us be like Saint Paul.

Group 1: Help us listen to you as Paul did.

All: **Help us, O Lord.**

Group 2: Help us tell people about your love.

All: **Help us, O Lord.**

Group 1: Help us be signs of your love to others.

All: **Help us, O Lord.**

Leader: Lord Jesus, thank you for the gift of your missionaries.

All: **Thank you, Lord. Amen.**

Leader: Let us pray.

Bow your heads as the leader prays.

All: **Amen.**

Sing together.

Their message
goes out through
all the earth.

"Psalm 19: Their Message Goes Out"

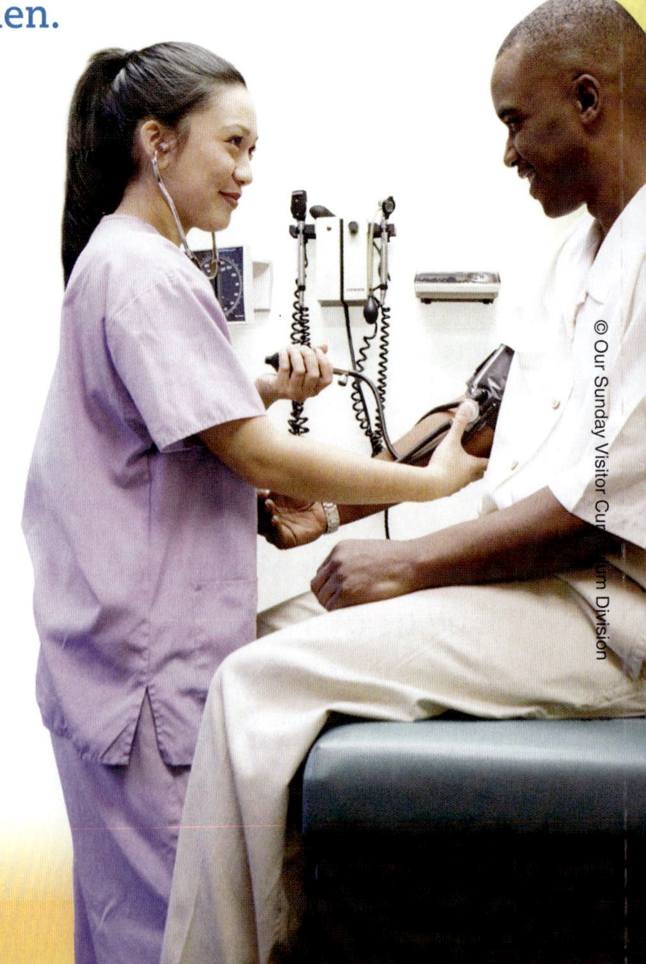

Choose Love

Leader: Loving God, guide us with your law of love.
"The law of the LORD is perfect,
refreshing the soul."
Psalm 19:8

All: Loving God, guide us with your law of love. Amen.

Activity Let's Begin

Which One?
Pretty boxes wrapped in paper.
Pick one box to open later.
Which to choose? Which to leave?
Can you guess which one will please?

- Tell which present you would choose. Give a reason for your choice.

Learning to Forgive

How did Joseph show forgiveness?

Faith Fact

Joseph had eleven brothers.

Choosing which present to open is easy. During your life you will have to make much harder choices. This letter tells the story of a man who made a difficult choice after he was separated from his family. It is based on a story from the Old Testament.

A LETTER

Joseph's Father and Brothers

Dear Father,

I hope this letter finds you well. I have great news for you. I am your son Joseph, and I am alive!

Long ago, you sent me to help my brothers tend your sheep. They were jealous because you loved me so much, so my brothers sold me as a slave. Then they told you that I was dead.

I was a slave in Egypt. I was put in charge of storing and giving out food because I worked hard and could explain dreams. One day, when the family needed food, you sent my brothers to Egypt to ask for it. They did not recognize me because so many years had passed.

At first, I did not tell them who I was. I was still angry with them. Then they told me that you were alive. I left the room

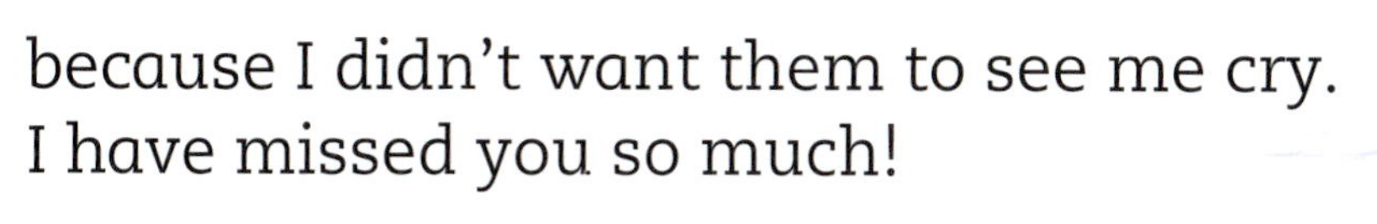

because I didn't want them to see me cry. I have missed you so much!

Finally, I told them who I was. They were surprised and happy. I have forgiven them, and I hope that you will, too.

Love,
Joseph

❓ **How do you think Joseph felt when he saw his brothers again?**

❓ **What other choices could Joseph have made?**

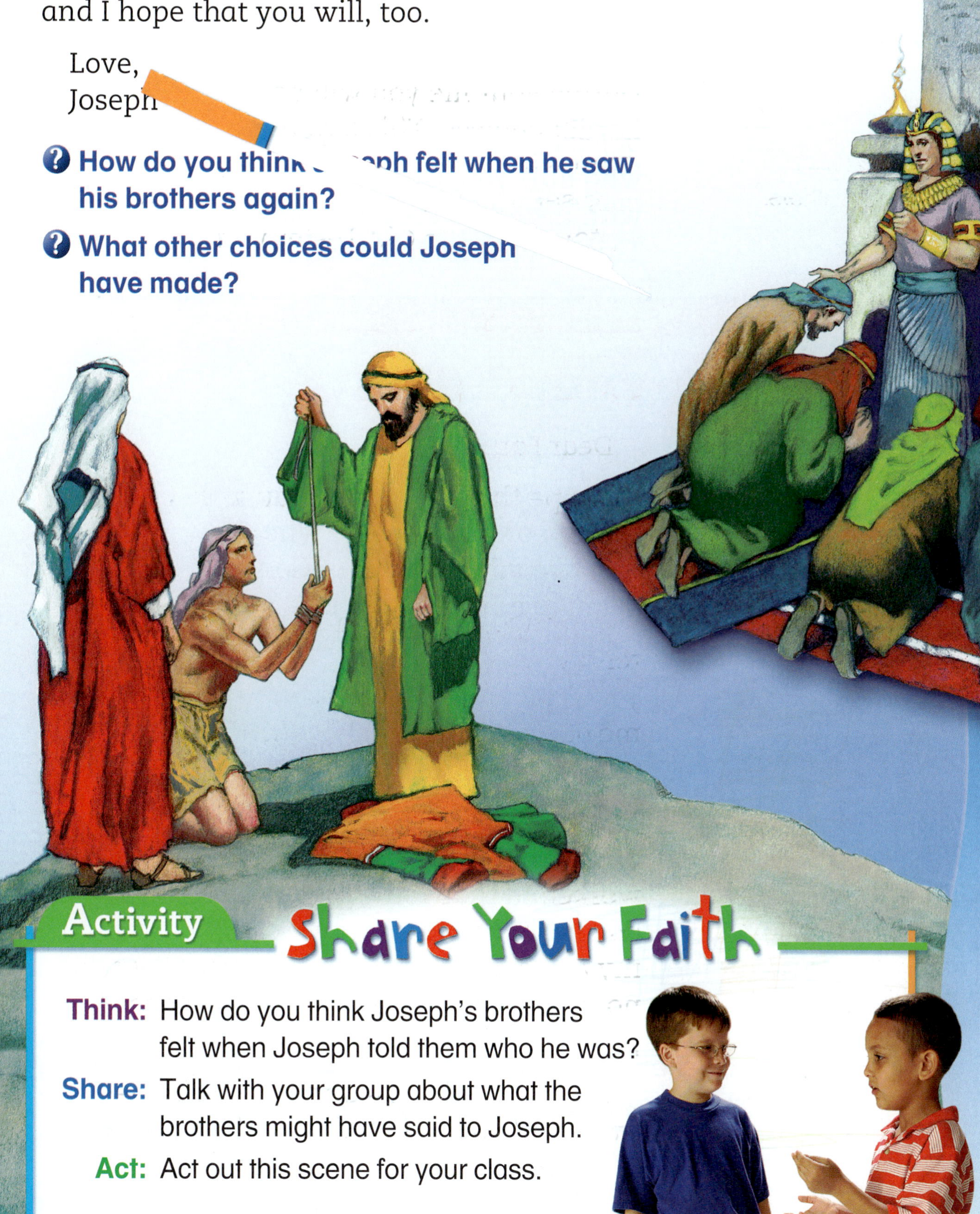

Activity Share Your Faith

Think: How do you think Joseph's brothers felt when Joseph told them who he was?

Share: Talk with your group about what the brothers might have said to Joseph.

Act: Act out this scene for your class.

Explore

Love One Another

Why do you need to be loving and forgiving?

Joseph chose to forgive his brothers because he loved them. Long before the time of Jesus, Joseph showed how to love those who hurt you. One day, Jesus was talking with his followers about how to treat people. This is what he told them.

SCRIPTURE Matthew 5:43–48

Love Your Enemy

You have been told to love your friends and hate your enemies. But now I am telling you: Love your enemies, and pray for people who hurt you. This will make you children of God. God doesn't want you to do only what is easy. If you are friendly only to people who are friendly to you, why is that special? People who know nothing about God do that. You must be perfect as God is perfect.

Based on *Matthew 5:43–48*

Jesus said that it is easier to love those who love you. He also said that you must love your enemies! That can be as difficult for people as it was for Joseph to forgive his brothers.

? Have you ever acted in a hurtful way towards others?

? What are some ways that you can live out Jesus' teaching?

The Law of Love

Jesus' main teachings are about the love and care you are called to show to others. In a teaching called the **Beatitudes**, Jesus said that those who make peace and show mercy are blessed by God. Jesus' **law of love** sums up the Ten Commandments and the Beatitudes in one statement: "Love one another. As I have loved you, so you also should love one another" *(John 13:34)*.

Living the Law of Love

People in your parish try to live by Jesus' law of love, too. There are probably volunteers who build houses, teach people to read, or give food to people who are hungry. They work for peace and justice wherever there is need. They go out of their way to show their love.

How can Jesus' law of love help you make good decisions?

Words of Faith

The **Beatitudes** are teachings of Jesus that show the way to true happiness and tell how to live in God's kingdom.

Jesus' **law of love** sums up the Ten Commandments and the Beatitudes in one statement.

Activity Connect Your Faith

Find the Answer Solve this puzzle to learn a lesson about love. Put the correct code letter in each blank to answer the question.

G	O	D	N	E	I	G	H	B	O	R	E	N	E	M	Y
1	2	3	4	5	6	7	8	9	10	11	12	13	14	15	16

What do these three words have in common?

W E (5) A R E (11 14) CALL E D (12 3)

T O (2) L O V E (10 12) T H E M. (8 14 15)

Prayer of Petition

Gather and begin with the Sign of the Cross.

Leader: God our Father, help us love as Jesus did.

Reader: When someone is mean to us, as Joseph's brothers were to him,

All: **Help us forgive as Joseph did.**

Reader: When we find it difficult to love,

All: **Help us love as Jesus did.**

Leader: We pray together an Act of Love.

All: **O God, we love you above all things, with our whole heart and soul, because you are all-good and worthy of all love. We love our neighbor as ourselves for love of you. We forgive all who have injured us and ask pardon of all whom we have injured.**

Leader: Let us pray.

Bow your heads as the leader prays.

All: **Amen.**

Sing together.

Love one another. Love one another, as I have loved you.

Care for each other. Care for each other, as I care for you.

CHAPTER 13

Review and Apply

A Check Understanding Put these events from the story of Joseph in order by numbering the sentences correctly.

4 Joseph recognizes his brothers and tells them who he is.

2 The brothers sell Joseph as a slave.

1 Joseph is loved by his father. His brothers are jealous.

5 Joseph forgives his brothers.

3 Joseph does well in Egypt. His brothers come to him for food.

B Make Connections How do you follow Jesus' law of love?

____

____

____

Activity Live Your Faith

Give Advice Write an advice column for a newspaper. On a separate sheet of paper, make up a problem that a reader might have in your school or neighborhood. Tell how Jesus' law of love would help make things better.

Family Faith

Catholics Believe

- Jesus' law of love is to love one another as Jesus loves each of us.
- Jesus teaches that we should love and forgive our enemies.

SCRIPTURE

I Corinthians 13:1–7 is about the meaning of loving. Think about different ways you can show your love for each family member.

www.osvcurriculum.com
For weekly scripture readings and seasonal resources

Activity

Live Your Faith

Make a Reminder Copy Jesus' law of love onto a decorative plaque, and hang it in your home where all will see it every day. Each week, sit down and review the past week, asking yourselves how well you have lived up to this central teaching of Jesus.

▲ Blessed Bartholomew Osypiuk 1844–1874

People of Faith

Bartholomew Osypiuk was an Eastern Catholic martyr killed in Pratulin, Poland. Bartholomew was married and the father of two children. He and his friends were killed by Russian soldiers because they refused to follow the ruler's commands about religion. The soldiers shot Bartholomew, but he forgave them before he died.

Family Prayer

Merciful God, help us learn to forgive our enemies as Bartholomew Osypiuk did. Amen.

In Unit 5 your child is learning about MORALITY.

CCC *See Catechism of the Catholic Church 1970, 1933 for further reading on chapter content.*

Chapter 14 Share Your Light

Let Us Pray

Leader: God our Creator, help us be a light in the darkness.

"Send your light and fidelity,
that they may be my guide."

Psalm 43:3

All: God our Creator, help us be a light in the darkness. Amen.

Activity Let's Begin

Candle

Brilliant, small
Flaming, flickering, dancing
Gives comfort
Friend in the night

- How can you be like a candle for others?

Be a Light

Focus How can you be a light to others?

The candle you were given at Baptism shows that you are a light for the world.

A candle brings light and comfort. This is a true story about a young girl who was a comforting light for others.

A STORY

Abbie's Light

"I have to go get supplies. Do you have any questions about the lighthouse?" asked Abbie's father.

"No. But I worry about keeping the light on in a storm," Abbie said.

"Just do your best. I have faith in you," said her father as he left.

That afternoon, a storm came, and it lasted for weeks. Every day Abbie made sure that the light was shining so that ships could find their way through the storm.

Finally, the storm ended. Her father returned. The two hugged each other. "I knew you could do this job well. I am so proud of you!" Abbie's father said.

? What did Abbie's father mean when he said he had faith in her?

The Light of the World

Abbie's light helped people at sea find their way to shore. Jesus talked about how people should help others find their way. One day Jesus told his followers what the world needed from them.

SCRIPTURE Matthew 5:14–16

Your Light Must Shine

"You are the light of the world," Jesus said. "A city on a mountaintop cannot be hidden."

He went on, "Nor do you light a lamp and then put it under a bushel basket; it is set on a lampstand, where it gives light to all in the house."

Finally he said, "Your light must shine before others, that they may see your good deeds and glorify your heavenly Father."

Based on *Matthew 5:14–16*

? Who has shared the light of Christ with you?

Activity Share Your Faith

Think: What good deeds have you performed lately?

Share: With your group, discuss ways you have shared the light of Christ with someone.

Act: Cut out paper flames and write one of your good deeds on each flame. Glue the flames to a piece of poster board.

Explore

The Virtues

Focus **What guides you through life?**

In some ways, Abbie's story is about the **virtues**—the habits of faith, hope, and love.

To have faith in someone is to believe in that person. Abbie's father believed that she could keep the light burning.

As a follower of Jesus, you believe in him. True faith is believing in God and all that God has said and done, even though you do not understand completely.

All through the storm, Abbie hoped that her father would come home. Hope is the virtue that helps you trust in what God has revealed. The Church hopes for a world that is more like God's kingdom.

What helps you stay hopeful during difficult times?

Love

When Abbie kept the light burning, she did a loving thing for the people at sea. You show your love for God by loving others. You help people. You listen to friends who have problems. The Church helps you show love for God by teaching you how to treat everyone with kindness and respect.

Words of Faith

Virtues are good qualities, or habits of goodness. The theological virtues of faith, hope, and love are gifts from God.

Practicing Virtues

In order to get better at something, you need to practice. You have to practice virtues until they become habits. When you do, these gifts from God—faith, hope, and love—grow strong in you.

How have you shown faith, hope, or love this week?

Activity — Connect Your Faith

Create a Reminder On a separate sheet of paper, design a bookmark about practicing one of the virtues as you share the light of Christ with others. Use the bookmark to remind yourself about practicing the virtues.

HOPE

Prayer of Petition

Gather and begin with the Sign of the Cross.

Leader: We pray together, asking Jesus to help us grow in faith, hope, and love.

All: **We know you, and so we have faith in you, O Jesus.**

Reader 1: Help us act with love toward one another.

Reader 2: Help us share the light of your love.

Reader 3: Give us the hope of living with you in heaven.

All: **Amen.**

Leader: Let us pray.

Bow your heads as the leader prays.

All: **Amen.**

Sing together.

This little light of mine I'm gonna let it shine,
This little light of mine I'm gonna let it shine;
This little light of mine I'm gonna let it shine,
Let it shine, let it shine, let it shine.

"This Little Light of Mine": African-American spiritual

Chapter 15

The Church Guides

Invite

Let Us Pray

Leader: God, please help me follow you.
"Guide me in your truth and teach me,
for you are God my savior."
Psalm 25:5

All: God, please help me follow you. Amen.

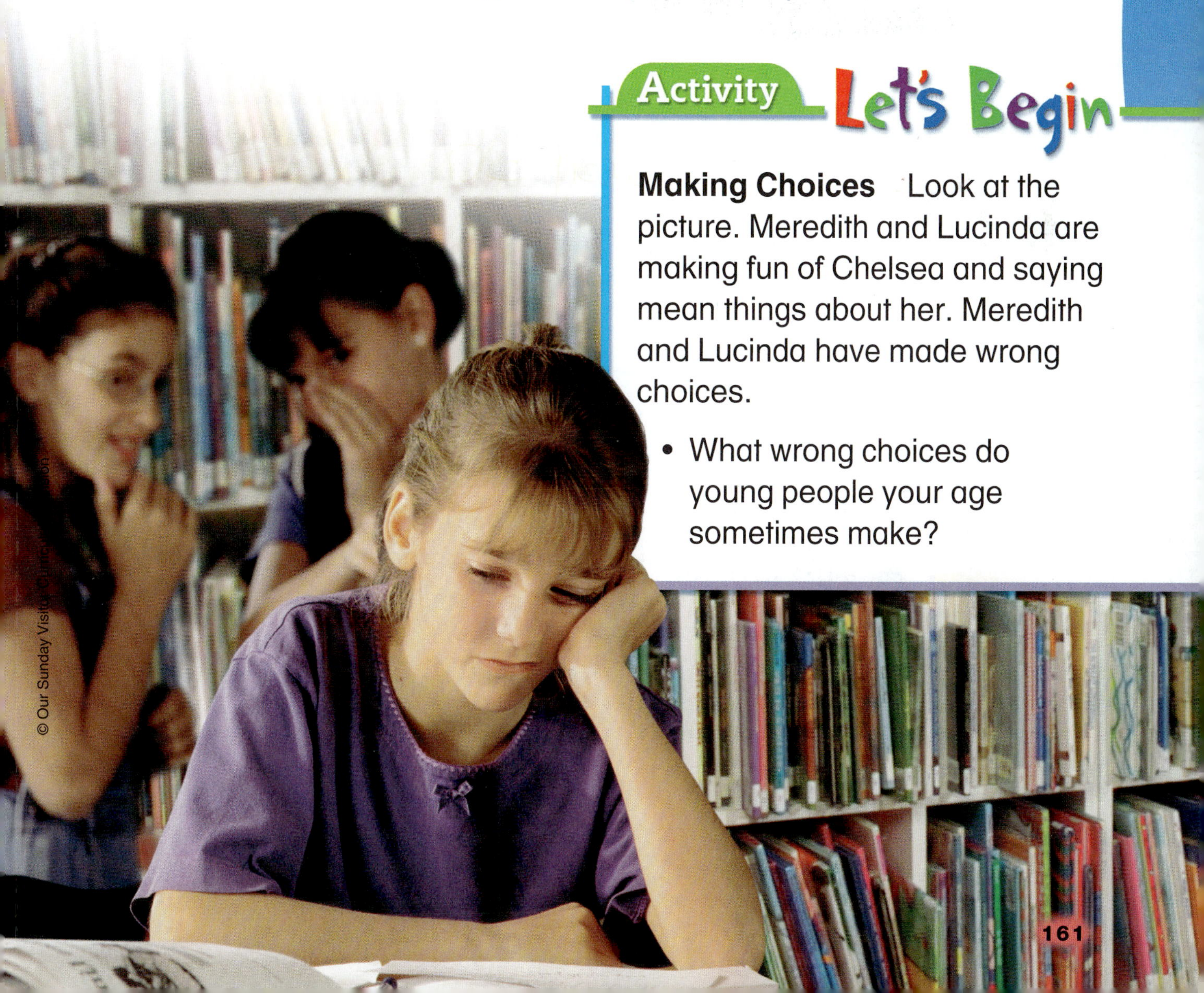

Activity Let's Begin

Making Choices Look at the picture. Meredith and Lucinda are making fun of Chelsea and saying mean things about her. Meredith and Lucinda have made wrong choices.

- What wrong choices do young people your age sometimes make?

Explore

Make Good Choices

How can someone who has sinned change?

Whenever you make a wrong choice, you must do something to make things right again. This is a story of someone who made a choice to think only of himself.

A STORY

The Selfish Giant

Once there was a giant who lived in a beautiful garden. The giant wanted the garden all to himself. He built a wall around it so that no one could get in.

One day, a child entered through a crack in the wall and climbed a tree. The tree burst into flowers, and birds came to nest in it.

The giant was awakened by the birds' song. "Who are you, and what have you done to my garden?" he called to the boy in the tree.

"I only climbed the tree. Then the flowers and birds came. I'm sorry if I hurt something," the boy said.

What would be a good ending for this story?

Change Your Life

This scripture story is about someone who changed for the better.

SCRIPTURE Acts 9:1–30

Saul and Jesus

Shortly after his Resurrection, Jesus returned to his Father. A man named Saul began turning in followers of Jesus to the authorities.

One day Saul was traveling between towns. A bright light flashed around him. He heard a voice say, "Saul, Saul, why are you persecuting me?"

Saul asked, "Who are you?"

The voice answered, "I am Jesus. Go into the city and do what you are told to do."

Saul did as Jesus said. He was baptized and became a great Christian preacher and writer. He is now known as Saint Paul, his other name.

Based on *Acts 9:1–30*

Activity Share Your Faith

Think: How do you think Saul felt when Jesus was talking to him?

Share: Talk about Saul's feelings with your group.

Act: With your group, create a mime to show how Saul's face and body changed as he was touched by the light of Jesus.

Explore

Guides for Living

Who and what can help you make good moral choices?

At times, everyone needs help to make good choices. The Holy Spirit helps you. God's **grace** in the sacraments can help you. Parents, priests, and teachers can help you form your **conscience**. The Church, through its teachings, also helps. The **precepts** are the basic laws of the church.

Precepts of the Church

Precept	How Each Precept Guides You
1. Take part in Mass on Sundays and holy days. Keep these days holy, and avoid unnecessary work.	Makes sure that you take time to be with Jesus and your parish community, strengthens your faith, rests your body, and encourages you to enjoy the world God has given you
2. Celebrate the Sacrament of Reconciliation at least once a year if there is serious sin.	Helps you look at your life to see how you need God's forgiveness and which actions you need to improve
3. Receive Holy Communion at least once a year during Easter time.	Strengthens your faith and makes you one with Jesus
4. Fast and abstain on days of penance.	Helps you share in the sacrifice of Jesus, train yourself spiritually, and experience the hunger of people who are poor
5. Give your time, gifts, and money to support the Church.	Encourages you to support the Church and participate in its works

Choices

Like the giant and Saul, everyone makes wrong choices at times. The deliberate choice to disobey God is called *sin*. When you sin, you hurt your relationship with God and other people.

You can experience God's forgiveness in the Sacrament of Reconciliation, also called Confession or Penance. Through the Sacrament of Reconciliation, the Church gives you a chance to take these actions:

- Look at what you have done.
- Say you are sorry, seek forgiveness, and receive absolution.
- Repair or make up for the wrong you have done, and change your behavior.

Why is the Sacrament of Reconciliation important?

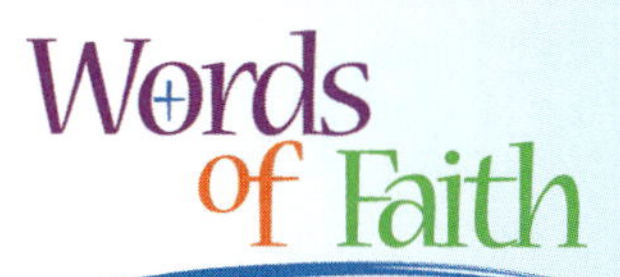

Grace is God's free and loving gift to humans of his own life and friendship.

Your **conscience** is a gift from God that helps you know the difference between right and wrong.

The **precepts of the Church** are some of the basic laws that Catholics should follow.

Activity Connect Your Faith

Talk It Over Form a "Decision Team" with several of your classmates. Talk about making good choices in the following situation, and list your choices in the space below.

- You can see your best friend's test paper from where you are sitting, and you know that she always gets the highest grade.

____

____

____

Prayer for Forgiveness

Gather and begin with the Sign of the Cross.

Sing together.

Lord, let your mercy be on us,
as we place our trust in you.

Leader: God our Loving Father, we come to you to ask forgiveness. Sometimes we have not behaved as we should.

Leader: If we have quarreled and called each other names,

All: **Sing the refrain.**

Leader: If we are lazy at home and in school,

All: **Sing the refrain.**

Leader: If we have not done good for others when we had the chance,

All: **Sing the refrain.**

Leader: Let us pray.

Bow your heads as the leader prays.

All: Amen.

Based on the
Rite of Penance

Chapter 16

Sacraments of Initiation

Leader: Loving God, help us answer your call.
"Sing to the LORD a new song,
a hymn in the assembly of the faithful."
Psalm 149:1

All: Loving God, help us answer your call. Amen.

Activity Let's Begin

Butterfly

Unseen within its silent shell
A life is stirring there,
Till one day wings emerge to beat
And loft into the air.
Now Caterpillar's gone away
And Monarch brightly greets
the day.

- What signs of life have you seen today?

New Life

How do you become a member of the Catholic Church?

Faith Fact

The Easter Vigil is celebrated on Holy Saturday.

The caterpillar gains new life as a butterfly. Most people receive new life in God when they are baptized as babies. This story is about an adult who found new life in Christ.

A STORY

New Life Begins

Brad's family was watching a videotape of the Easter Vigil celebration.

Aunt Stella and the other adults celebrated three sacraments in one evening. First, they were baptized. Then, they were anointed with the blessed oil called **chrism**. Finally, they received Holy Communion.

After Mass, everyone was laughing and hugging Aunt Stella and the others. Brad enjoyed all the excitement, and he looked very happy on the videotape!

How does your family celebrate new beginnings?

Life in the Church

After they saw the videotape, the family looked at a photo album. "Look, Brad," his sister Krista said. "Here are pictures of your Baptism. And here you are on your First Communion day."

The family noticed some differences between the celebrations. Brad had been baptized as a baby at the baptismal font, but Aunt Stella had stepped into the baptismal pool. Baby Brad had worn a white baptismal gown, but Aunt Stella wore a white robe. Brad received First Communion for the first time in second grade. Stella was an adult, and she received Eucharist on the same day she was baptized.

Still, some things were the same. Brad's godfather was Aunt Stella's sponsor, too. Father Russell had baptized both Brad and Aunt Stella.

Brad's mom smiled. "Now we're not only members of the Gordon family—we're all members of the same Church family, too."

Words of Faith

Chrism is the blessed oil used in the Sacraments of Baptism, Confirmation, and Holy Orders.

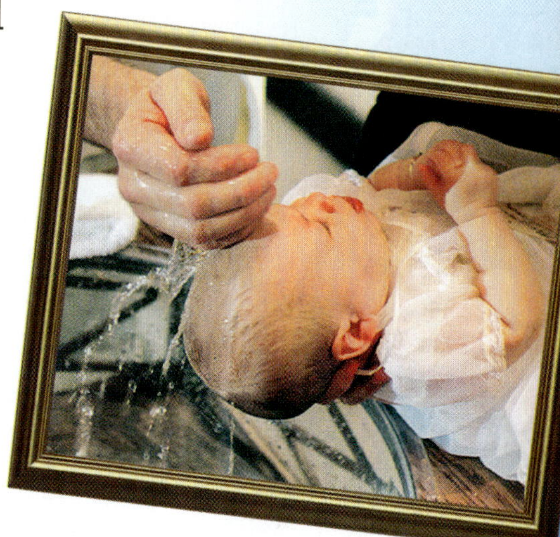

Share Your Faith

Think: Remember the day of your First Communion.

Share: Tell your small group about this special day.

Act: Draw a picture about one of the stories you heard in your group.

Gifts from God

What do the Sacraments of Initiation mean?

Aunt Stella celebrated three sacraments at the Easter Vigil. **Sacraments** are signs that come from Jesus and give grace, God's life in people. Through the power of the Holy Spirit, Jesus works in and through the sacraments.

SCRIPTURE Acts 2:38–41

Many Are Baptized

After the Holy Spirit came to Jesus' followers at Pentecost, Peter told those who were gathered what they should do.

Peter said to the crowd, "Repent and be baptized, every one of you, in the name of Jesus Christ for the forgiveness of your sins; and you will receive the gift of the holy Spirit."

Peter told the people that Jesus' promise was meant for everyone. Many of them accepted his message. About 3,000 people were baptized that day.

Based on *Acts 2:38–41*

Members of the Church community are changed through the sacraments. Baptism, Confirmation, and Eucharist are called the **Sacraments of Initiation**, or beginning.

Sharing God's Love

In each of the Sacraments of Initiation, you see the actions and hear the words of the minister, who acts in the name of the Holy Trinity. The Son, by the power of the Holy Spirit, shares with you the love of the Father.

Sacraments are signs that come from Jesus and give grace.

The **Sacraments of Initiation** are Baptism, Confirmation, and Eucharist. They celebrate membership in the Catholic Church.

Sacraments of Initiation

	Words and Actions	Effects
Baptism	The priest or deacon pours water on or immerses the person, saying, "I baptize you in the name of the Father, and of the Son, and of the Holy Spirit."	Removes original sin, forgives personal sin, and gives new life in Christ; marks the person as a member of Christ's Body, the Church; unites all Christians
Confirmation	The bishop or priest lays hands on the person's head and then anoints him or her with chrism, saying, "Be sealed with the Gift of the Holy Spirit."	Seals and completes Baptism; strengthens the person's bond with the Church; unites the person more fully with Christ; strengthens him or her in living the faith
Eucharist	The priest prays the Eucharistic Prayer, consecrating bread and wine; then he shares Christ's Body and Blood with the Church community.	Brings forgiveness of venial sins and an increase of grace; unites all who share the Eucharist into the one Body of Christ

Activity Connect Your Faith

Show Welcome In the space below, draw a picture of your Church family welcoming a new member.

Pray with God's Word

Gather and begin with the Sign of the Cross.

Leader: God our Father, help us always live out the promises of our Baptism, just as Jesus did.

Reader 1: A reading from the Gospel according to Mark.

Read Mark 1:9–11.

Reader 2: Jesus went to the Jordan River from Nazareth.

Reader 3: He was baptized by John.

Reader 1: When he came out of the water, the Spirit came down from the sky in the form of a dove.

Reader 2: The Gospel of the Lord.

All: Praise to you, Lord Jesus Christ.

Leader: Let us pray.

Bow your head as the leader prays.

All: Amen.

Sing together.

Christ will be your strength!

Learn to know and follow him!

"Christ Will Be Your Strength" © 1988, GIA Publications, Inc.

Review and Apply

Check Understanding Circle the correct answer. Correct any false statements.

1. Which of the following is NOT a Sacrament of Initiation?
   - a. Baptism
   - b. Eucharist
   - c. Holy Orders
   - d. Confirmation
2. What is chrism?
   - a. blessed oil used during certain sacraments
   - b. a Communion wafer
   - c. a prayer
3. Sacraments are signs of grace.

   True False ______________________
4. Singing hymns brings forgiveness of venial sins and an increase of grace.

   True False ______________________
5. Confirmation strengthens your bond with your parents.

   True False ______________________

Activity Live Your Faith

Create Make a booklet about the sacraments you have celebrated. Include drawings, photographs, or writing by you and other members of your family.

Family Faith

Catholics Believe

- Sacraments are signs that come from Jesus and give grace.
- The Sacraments of Initiation are Baptism, Confirmation, and Eucharist.

SCRIPTURE

Acts 2:17 is about gifts from God. Read the verse and talk about what it means for your family.

GO online www.osvcurriculum.com
For weekly scripture readings and seasonal resources

Activity

Live Your Faith

Welcome New Members Find out who in your parish is preparing for the Sacraments of Initiation. Choose a way to help one of the catechumens feel more welcome in your parish. For example, you and other families could invite a catechumen and his or her family to a potluck dinner at one of your homes.

▲ Saint Isaac Jogues 1607–1644

People of Faith

Isaac Jogues was a priest and an explorer in North America. He became a priest in France and was sent to Canada in 1636. He spent six years preaching the gospel. Isaac was held captive by Native Americans in New York. He was freed by Dutch settlers but continued his mission in Canada. A hostile group of Native Americans killed him. His feast day is October 19.

Family Prayer

Saint Isaac, pray for us that we may understand and believe in our work for the Church's mission. Help us bring God's love to others. Amen.

In Unit 6 your child is learning about SACRAMENTS.
CCC *See Catechism of the Catholic Church 1131–1132, 1212, 1271 for further reading on chapter content.*

Let Us Pray

Leader: O God, give me strength.
"O Lord, my God,
I cried out to you and you healed me."
Psalm 30:3

All: O God, give me strength. Amen.

Activity Let's Begin

Making Things Right Russell and his Uncle Anton were working on his bike. "I had the worst day ever," Russell said. "I told Carlos that Amelia said his art project looked dumb. Amelia found out, and now they're both mad at me. How can I make things right?"

"It won't be as easy as oiling this chain," Uncle Anton replied.

- What can Russell do about his problem?

Explore

Jesus Heals

How can faith lead to healing?

During his life, Jesus helped make things right for many people. He healed people who had faith in him. Read the story about Jesus healing a man's daughter. The scene begins with a crowd standing around Jesus as he teaches.

SCRIPTURE Luke 8:40–42, 49–56

Jesus Gives New Life

Jairus: Please let me through. I must talk to Jesus.

Woman: You look worried. Stand aside. Let this man through to see Jesus.

Jairus: Jesus, please. I beg you to come to my home. My only daughter is dying.

Jairus's servant: Jairus, I have sad news. Your daughter is dead.

Jesus: Jairus, don't be afraid. Have faith, and your daughter will be all right.

Jairus's wife: Jesus, thank you for coming to our home. Everyone is sad because our daughter just died.

Jesus: She isn't dead. She is sleeping. Now everyone except her parents and my three friends must leave.

Crowd: He doesn't know what he's talking about. She really is dead!

Jesus: [touching the girl] Child, wake up!

[The girl wakes up; her parents hug her.]

Jesus: Please don't tell anyone what I did here today.

Jairus's wife: Thank you so much, Jesus! You have given us back our daughter.

Based on *Luke 8:40–42, 49–56*

Activity Share Your Faith

Think: Reflect on the story of the healing of Jairus's daughter.

Share: How do you think Jairus felt after Jesus healed his daughter?

Act: With a group of classmates, act out the story. Tell how you felt when you played your part.

Explore

Sacraments of Healing

How do the Sacraments of Healing help Christians?

The **Sacraments of Healing** are Reconciliation, or Penance, and the Anointing of the Sick. These sacraments help people in times of sin or sickness.

During Reconciliation you confess your sins and are forgiven. In the Anointing of the Sick, the priest prays that God will send his healing love to the person who is being anointed. This sacrament shows that every person is special and that life is sacred.

Only a priest can preside at the Sacraments of Healing. Like all sacraments, these sacraments use words and actions to show God's love.

Have you ever been present at the Anointing of the Sick?

Signs of Healing

Sacrament	Action	Words
Reconciliation	The priest extends his hand in blessing.	"I absolve you from your sins in the name of the Father, and of the Son, and of the Holy Spirit."
Anointing of the Sick	The priest uses the oil of the sick to anoint the head and hands of the person who is very sick or aged.	"Through this holy anointing may the Lord in his love and mercy help you with the grace of the Holy Spirit. May the Lord who frees you from sin save you and raise you up."

Sin and Sickness

Sin and sickness are different in a very important way. Sickness may separate you from others, but you do not choose to be sick. However, when you sin, you make a choice to turn away from God and others; and you are responsible for that decision.

The Church Cares

The effects of sin and sickness can be similar. Both can make you feel separated from God and from people you love. The Sacraments of Healing allow the community a chance to share your sorrows and joys. These sacraments show that the Church cares about people. The Church prays for Jesus' spiritual and physical healing.

Words of Faith

The **Sacraments of Healing** are Reconciliation and the Anointing of the Sick. In these sacraments God's forgiveness and healing are given to those suffering physical and spiritual sickness.

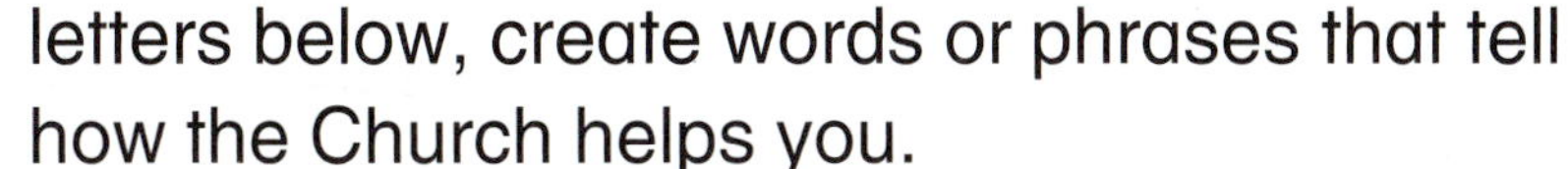

Activity — Connect Your Faith

Use Healing Words Sin and sickness often separate you in some way from those you love. Using the letters below, create words or phrases that tell how the Church helps you.

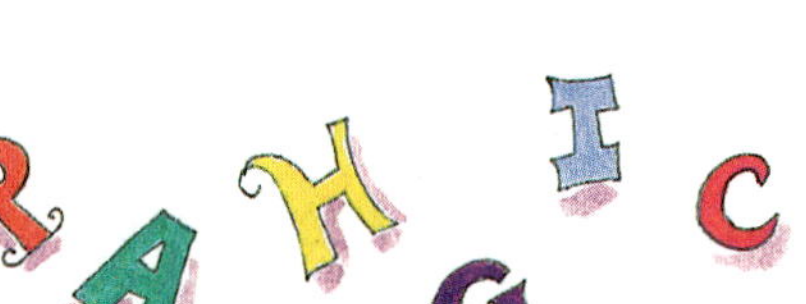

____

____

Prayer for Healing

Gather and begin with the Sign of the Cross.

Leader: God wants us to ask for what we need in prayer. We pray now for those people we know who need God's healing.

Reader 1: Loving God, you take every family under your care.

Reader 2: You know our physical and spiritual needs.

All: **Strengthen us with your grace so that we may grow in faith and love.**

Reader 1: We ask this through our Lord Jesus Christ, your Son,

Reader 2: Who lives and reigns with you and the Holy Spirit.

All: **One God, for ever and ever. Amen.**

Based on a prayer from the Rite of the Anointing of the Sick

Sing together.

Amazing grace! how sweet the sound,
That saved a wretch like me! I once was lost, but now am found, Was blind, but now I see.

"Amazing Grace" St. 1–4, John Newton; St. 5, attr. to John Rees

CHAPTER 17

Review and Apply

Check Understanding Circle True if a statement is true, and circle False if a statement is false. Correct any false statements.

1. Faith in Jesus' healing power was important in the story of Jairus's daughter.

   True False ______________________________

2. Eucharist is a Sacrament of Healing.

   True False ______________________________

3. The Sacraments of Healing help people physically and spiritually.

   True False ______________________________

4. Oil is used for the Anointing of the Sick.

   True False ______________________________

5. Both sickness and sin separate you from God.

   True False ______________________________

Activity Live Your Faith

Pray for Others Make a list of people who are ill or have other needs. Choose one of the people, and pray to God for that person once each day for five days.

Family Faith

Catholics Believe

- The Sacraments of Healing are Reconciliation and the Anointing of the Sick.
- In these sacraments the Church prays for spiritual and physical healing.

SCRIPTURE

James 5:13–15 was written about the Anointing of the Sick and the forgiveness of sin.

GO online **www.osvcurriculum.com**
For weekly scripture readings and seasonal resources

Activity

Live Your Faith

Show Your Love As a family, as often as possible, visit relatives, friends, and neighbors who are ill or aged. If you cannot visit the people who need your help, call the person or show your love by sending homemade cards.

People of Faith

▲ Saint Elizabeth of Hungary 1207–1231

Elizabeth was a princess of Hungary who married Prince Ludwig of Germany. She cared for people who were poor and suffering. At the castle gate, Elizabeth fed those who were poor. She sold her jewels and used the money to build hospitals. Before she died, she gave her belongings to people who were poor. Saint Elizabeth's feast day is November 17.

Family Prayer

Saint Elizabeth, pray for us that we may be kind to people who are poor and sick. Amen.

In Unit 6 your child is learning about SACRAMENTS.

 CCC *See Catechism of the Catholic Church 1420, 1421 for further reading on chapter content.*

Sacraments of Service

Invite

Let Us Pray

Leader: Dear God, we are your servants forever.
"The LORD redeems loyal servants;
no one is condemned whose refuge is God."

Psalm 34:23

All: Dear God, we are your servants forever. Amen.

Activity Let's Begin

A Special Day "Happy anniversary, Mom and Dad! We know today is special for you, so we made you breakfast," said Jeremy.

"Wow, what a feast!" Dad said.

"You always do special things for us. Now it's our turn to do something special for you," said Samantha.

- What special things do you do for your parents?

Family Memories

How do married people and ordained men serve others?

An anniversary is a time to remember a special day of love and commitment. Jeremy and Samantha learn about their parents' wedding day.

A STORY

The Wedding Story

"Mom, you looked pretty," Samantha said.

"It's because I was so happy," said her mother.

"I remember being happy because your mom and I were promising to be with each other forever and to share good and bad times," Dad said.

"I know it's fun to share good times. But bad times?" asked Samantha.

"Well, Samantha," said Mom, "everyone has bad times, but mine would be worse if I didn't have your dad. We often ask God to help us. The good times are even better because I share them with someone I love."

What good memories of weddings and married life have family members shared with you?

Sharing Wedding Memories

"Look, there's a picture of Father Schmidt, witnessing our wedding **vows**," said Mom. "He also met with us before we were married and talked to us about how important marriage is. He asked us to go to some special classes to learn more about marriage. Priests and deacons do a lot of work that you don't always see."

"What kind of work?" asked Jeremy.

"They teach people about the faith and guide them in making good decisions. They visit people who are sick and serve the parish in many other ways. Priests celebrate Mass and other sacraments. Deacons baptize and witness marriages. Priests and deacons have important roles," said Dad.

"Just like married people," said Samantha. "Yes, just like married people. God helps all of us do his work," said Mom.

Words of Faith

Vows are sacred promises that are made to or before God. In marriage a man and a woman make their promises to love each other and to be faithful before God.

Activity: Share Your Faith

Think: What is love?

Share: Talk about different meanings of love and how you can show love for others.

Act: Design an anniversary card about love, and give it to a friend or relative who is celebrating an anniversary.

Explore

Serving God's People

How do the Sacraments of Service continue Jesus' work?

The parents and the priest in the story had something in common. They had celebrated a **Sacrament of Service**. The two Sacraments of Service are Holy Orders and Matrimony.

Holy Orders is the sacrament in which men become deacons, priests, or bishops. When a man receives Holy Orders, he is ordained. He shares Jesus' ministry in a special way. Saint Paul wrote about the work of the Church's early ministers.

Think of us as servants of Christ and stewards of the mysteries of God. Stewards must be trustworthy.

Based on *I Corinthians 4:1–2*

Sacraments of Service

	Words and Actions	Effects
Matrimony	In front of a priest or deacon and other witnesses, a woman and a man promise to love each other and to be faithful.	The grace to love each other as Christ loves his Church and to remain faithful; the grace to welcome and raise children
Holy Orders (ordination to the priesthood)	A bishop lays his hands on the man to be ordained and prays to the Holy Spirit.	The authority to minister as a priest, with the authority to lead the Church community, to teach, and to govern

Serving One Another

Married people share Jesus' ministry, too. The Sacrament of Matrimony joins a man and a woman in Christian marriage. They serve God by loving and serving each other and any children they may have.

Sometimes both husbands and wives serve each other by working at jobs so that their families will have food and shelter.

Sometimes a man and a woman have to live apart from each other. However, they must still do the best they can to help their families. The Church cares for and supports all of these families.

Words of Faith

The **Sacraments of Service** are Holy Orders and Matrimony. They celebrate people's commitment to serve God and the community.

All Are Called

Through Baptism and Confirmation, all members of the Church are called to use their gifts in service to God's people. No matter how you answer that call, you serve God and strengthen the Church community.

Activity Connect Your Faith

Learn About Sacraments of Service In this space, write two questions that you would like to ask your pastor and a married person about how they serve.

____

____

Prayer of Thanks

Gather and begin with the Sign of the Cross.

Leader: Generous God, we thank you for the gifts of service of bishops, priests, deacons, and married people.

Reader 1: For priests who lead us to you,

All: **We thank you, God.**

Reader 2: For deacons who help us find you,

All: **We thank you, God.**

Reader 3: For bishops who guide your people,

All: **We thank you, God.**

Reader 4: For married people who lead each other to God,

All: **We thank you, God.**

Reader 5: For parents who show us how to love you,

All: **We thank you, God.**

Sing together.

Will you let me be
your servant,
Let me be as
Christ to you; Pray that I may have the grace to
Let you be my servant, too.

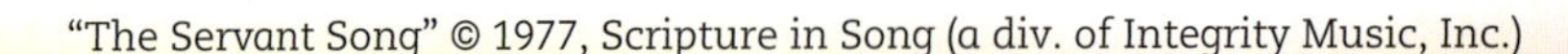
"The Servant Song" © 1977, Scripture in Song (a div. of Integrity Music, Inc.)

CHAPTER 18

Review and Apply

Check Understanding Complete each sentence with the correct term from the Word Bank.

1. A man must be ____________________ to celebrate the Mass.
2. The ____________________ made during the Sacraments of Service last a lifetime.
3. Only men are called to receive ____________________.
4. Holy Orders celebrates a man's commitment to Jesus' ministry as a ____________________, deacon, or bishop.
5. ____________________ unites a man and a woman.

WORD BANK

vows
Holy Orders
Matrimony
ordained
priest

Activity Live Your Faith

Write a List Brainstorm a list of things you can do to show your thanks for what the adults in your family do for you. Choose an idea that would surprise them completely, and act on it this week.

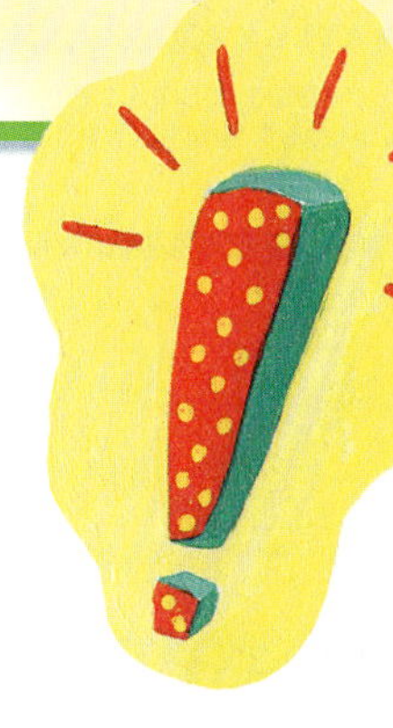

____

____

____

____

____

____

Family Faith

Catholics Believe

- The Sacraments of Service are Holy Orders and Matrimony.
- These sacraments celebrate people's commitment to God and the community.

SCRIPTURE

I Corinthians 13 tells you what love is and how important it is.

www.osvcurriculum.com
For weekly scripture readings and seasonal resources

Activity

Live Your Faith

Support Others Reach out to a family who may be having difficulties at this time. Decide what you can do to support that family. Here are some families you might be able to help.

- A family with a new baby or very young children
- A family experiencing a death or an illness
- An elderly couple with no children to look after them

People of Faith

▲ Saint Margaret of Scotland 1045–1093

Margaret was a princess who was shipwrecked with her family near Scotland. She married Malcolm, the king of Scotland. She brought great learning and compassion to the Scottish court. She helped orphans and served the needs of those who were poor. Margaret helped repair many church buildings in Scotland. Saint Margaret's feast day is November 16.

Family Prayer

Saint Margaret, pray for us that we may lead lives of service to our families, our country, and our Church. Amen.

In Unit 6 your child is learning about SACRAMENTS.

 CCC *See Catechism of the Catholic Church 1534, 1535 for further reading on chapter content.*

Unit 6 Review

A **Work with Words** Complete each statement.

1. ____________________ are sacred promises that are made to or before God.

2. Sacraments of ____________________ celebrate people's commitment to serve God and the community.

3. ____________________ are signs that come from Jesus and give grace.

4. Sacraments of ____________________ celebrate membership in the Catholic Church.

5. ____________________ is blessed oil used in some sacraments.

B **Check Understanding** Complete the chart below with the names of the sacraments.

Sacraments	
Initiation	**Healing**
6.	9.
7.	10.
8.	

Unit 7
Kingdom of God

In this unit you will...

learn that the Church is a sign of God's covenant. We share in the mission to work for peace and justice. In this way we are signs of God's kingdom. If we die in God's friendship, we will live forever in his presence. At the end of the world, Christ will judge all people by how they lived their lives.

What do you think you will learn in this unit about the kingdom of God?

Invite

Chapter 19 Belonging to God

Leader: Faithful God, help us follow your path to love.

"All the paths of the LORD are faithful love
toward those who honor the covenant
demands."

Psalm 25:10

All: Faithful God, help us follow your path to love.
Amen.

Activity Let's Begin

Those Who Came Before

"Wow, look at this arrowhead!" LaNae said.

"I wonder who made it," said Greg.

"Maybe we can find out about who lived here before the pioneers. That might give us clues about the arrowhead," Ms. Ortiz suggested.

- What are some ways to learn about the past in your family and in the Church?

Explore

Family History

What was God's covenant with Abraham?

The beginnings of the Church's history go back to ancient times. Here is the story of the time when God first called his people.

A STORY

I Will Be Your God

"Tell me about before I was born," said Isaac.

Sarah smiled. "Your father and I were sad. We had no children. One night your father went outside. When he came back, he said that he and God had been speaking.

"Your father said to God, 'You know that we trust you, but we have no children.'"

Isaac's mother continued, "God told your father to look up at the stars. God said, 'Your family will outnumber the stars. They will be my people, and I will be their God. All nations will be blessed through you. This is my **covenant**, my promise to you.'"

Isaac finished the story, "I share that promise, and so will my children."

What family stories do you enjoy hearing again and again?

Connected to the Past

God kept his promise. Abraham's family grew to be the people of Israel. God was faithful to the covenant.

Then Jesus, God's own Son, was born into a Jewish family. God extended the covenant to all people through Jesus' death and Resurrection. God's promise was fulfilled in Jesus. All people were saved from the power of sin and everlasting death through Jesus.

Followers of Jesus and members of the Church continue to be a sign of God's covenant. They do this as they proclaim the good news of Jesus and God's kingdom.

What was the covenant between God and the people of Israel?

A **covenant** is a sacred promise or agreement between God and humans.

Think: Think about God's promise to Abraham.

Share: Write on an index card a promise you will make with God.

Act: Keep the index card in your pocket to remind you of your own covenant with God.

Explore

The Church Through Time

Focus How did the Church grow?

Jesus and his first followers were Jews. After Jesus returned to the Father, some of his followers continued to attend Jewish services on the Sabbath. They also gathered to celebrate the Eucharist in their homes.

The followers of Christ became known as **Christians**. They saw themselves as a new people, as the Church. Christians spread the good news to other lands.

The early years of the Church were times of persecution, when many Christians were imprisoned or put to death. Even in difficult times, Jesus' followers remembered God's promises and tried to be faithful to him and to the covenant.

? Why is it important to learn about the early Christians?

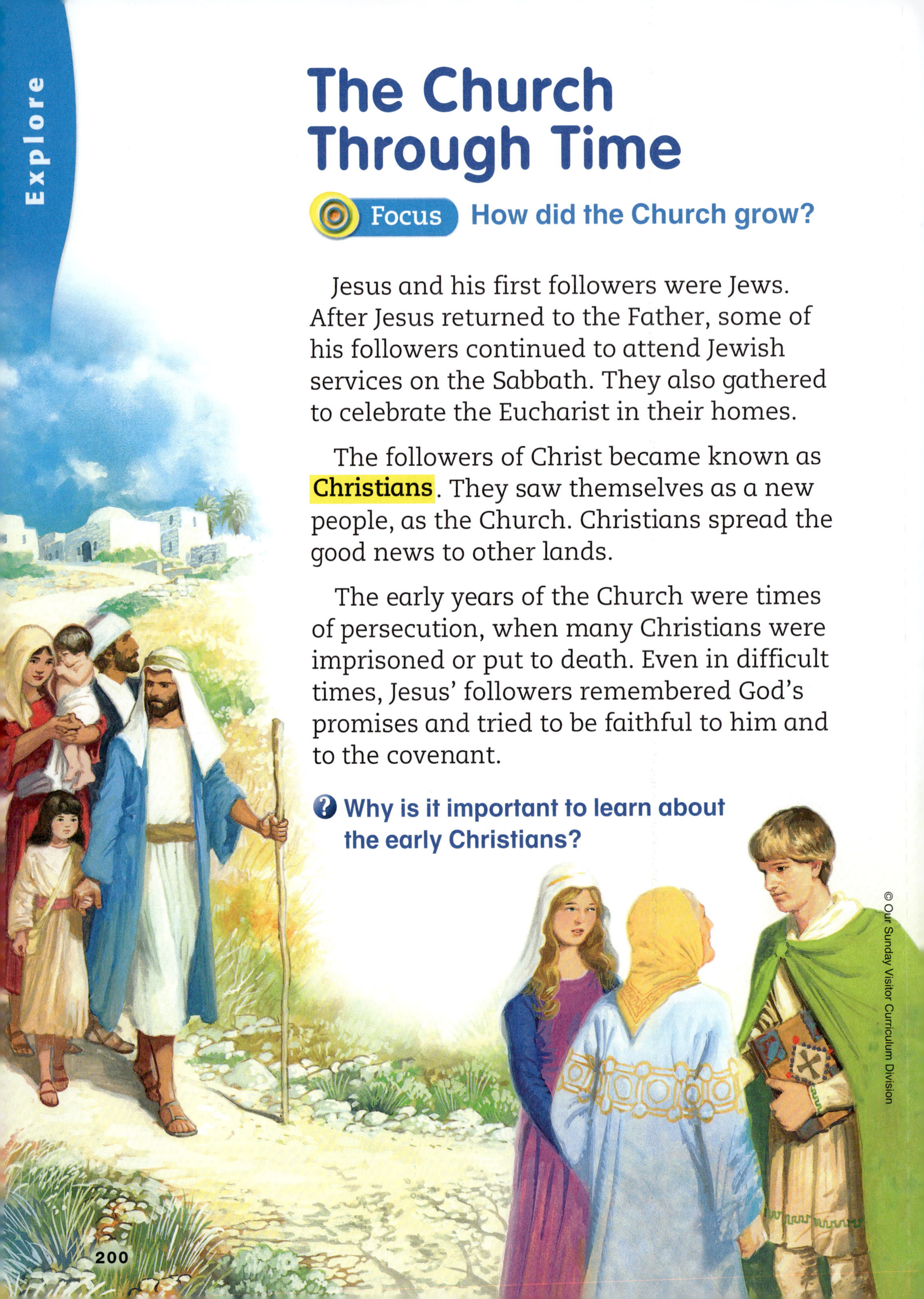

The Church Grows

Christians kept the Church alive and growing. When invaders from the North attacked Rome, Christians in Ireland and Scotland kept the gospel alive in monasteries. Saints including Patrick, Brigid, Kevin, and Columba carried on the Church's mission.

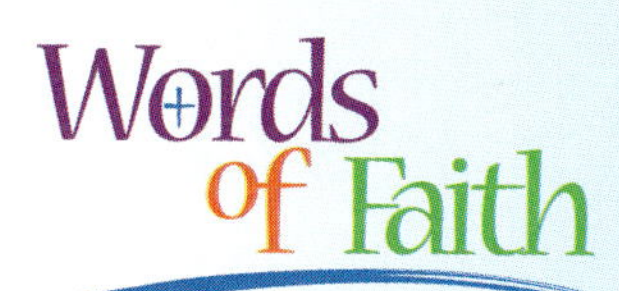

Christians are followers of Jesus Christ. The word *Christian* comes from *Christ*.

Into the Present

Many saints you have read about this year in People of Faith have bravely carried the word of God to distant lands. The Catholic faith has spread throughout Africa, Asia, Europe, and the Americas.

The Church's history is still being written today. You and all people who follow Jesus are an important part of the story of faith as well.

Activity

Describe Christians How do people know that you are a Christian?

People know that I am a follower of Jesus because

___

My parish family shows that it follows Jesus by

___

When I think of Catholic Christians, I think of

___

Celebrate

Prayer of Faith

Gather and begin with the Sign of the Cross.

Leader: God our Father, we remember today our ancestors who have walked in faith with you.

Reader 1: Faith is getting what we have hoped for. It is our hope of what we have not seen.

Reader 2: By faith we believe that God created the world.

Reader 3: By faith Noah built an ark when he could see no water.

Reader 1: By faith Abraham obeyed when God sent him to a faraway place.

Reader 2: By faith Moses led God's people across the Red Sea as if it were dry land.

Reader 3: Yet God had something even better for his people.

Based on *Hebrews 11*

All: **Thanks be to God.**

Sing together.

We are walking by faith, we are walking by faith, we are walking by faith to the kingdom! In prayer we will listen, in your wisdom we will grow; we will walk by faith till we come to the promised land!

Review and Apply

Work with Words Write or circle the correct response.

1. God (abandoned/was faithful to) the people of Israel.
2. Early Christians met to pray at Jewish services and in (homes/Catholic churches).
3. Early Christians (hid/shared) their faith and were sometimes persecuted for doing so.
4. What is a covenant?

   ____

5. What was God's covenant with Abraham and Sarah?

   ____

Activity Live Your Faith

Praise a Saint Recall a Christian saint who helped spread the word of God. Tell the saint's story in your own words or in pictures. Name one thing you can do to follow the example of that saint.

____

____

____

____

____

____

____

____

Family Faith

Catholics Believe

- God kept his promise to be forever faithful when he sent his Son, Jesus.
- The Church continues to be a sign of God's covenant.

SCRIPTURE

2 Corinthians 3:1–18 tells how the early Christians saw themselves as ministers.

GO online **www.osvcurriculum.com**
For weekly scripture readings and seasonal resources

Activity

Live Your Faith

Talk About Christian Living Read about the lives of the early Christians in *Acts 2:42–47* and *Acts 4:32–35*. Discuss how they lived and why you think it was important for the early Christians to live this way. List some ways in which your family and your parish community are like the early Christian community.

▲ Saint Clement of Rome died c. A.D. 100

People of Faith

Clement was one of Jesus' early followers. He became bishop of Rome and was one of the first popes. Clement worked hard to help the Church grow. He taught people by writing letters. Sometimes you hear his name during Mass. Saint Clement's feast day is November 23.

Family Prayer

Saint Clement, pray for us that we may stand up for our faith. Help us teach others about what is important to us as followers of Christ. Amen.

In Unit 7 your child is learning about the KINGDOM OF GOD.

CCC *See Catechism of the Catholic Church 781, 1612 for further reading on chapter content.*

Chapter 20 The Church Today

Let Us Pray

Leader: God our Creator, help us build up your Church.
"The stone the builders rejected
has become the cornerstone."
Psalm 118:22

All: God our Creator, help us build up your Church. Amen.

Activity Let's Begin

What Would You Do? "Imagine that you have the power to solve just one problem in the world," Sister Lorraine said. "Which problem would you choose?"

The children were silent for a moment. Then they started to make suggestions.

"I would end wars," Ernesto said.

"I would make sure that nobody was poor," Anna said.

"I would stop pollution," said Jen.

- Which problem would you choose to solve? Why?

Explore

The Work of the Church

What difference can one person make?

The world has many problems that need to be solved. The Church is working to solve these problems. Read this story about a girl who helped others.

A STORY

Colleen's Concert

Colleen spent her summer vacation planning a special event. She wanted to help people by holding a concert. She invited musicians to help. She chose music and found a leader for the band.

Colleen's concert was held on a summer evening in her neighborhood.

"I wanted people to enjoy the music, but I also wanted to make money to help fight an illness one of my friends has. We earned a lot of money, and we had fun," Colleen said. "Best of all, maybe the money will help scientists find a cure for an illness."

How did Colleen's concert make a difference in the world?

Doing Jesus' Work

Colleen worked hard to solve a problem. Jesus once sent out some of his followers to make a difference.

Matthew 10:5–14

Sending Out the Disciples

Jesus sent his followers on a mission to tell his good news and cure people who were sick. These are the instructions he gave them.

Travel to visit the people of Israel. Tell them that the kingdom of God is at hand. Cure people who are sick. Don't take supplies or extra clothes or sandals. Whenever you come to a town, find a good person's home, and stay there as long as you are in the town. When you go into a house, bless it. If people do not accept you or listen to you, leave the house or town and have nothing to do with it.

Based on *Matthew 10:5–14*

Share Your Faith

Think: What do you think Jesus' followers thought about his instructions?

Share: Talk with your group about how Jesus' followers felt.

Act: Make a collage about their mission. Share it with your class.

Help Today

How does the Church help others in the world today?

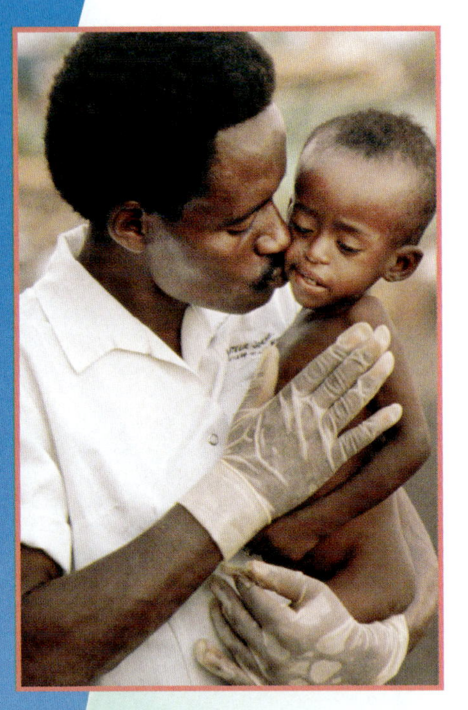

You know that there are many problems in the world. Some of the problems are so big that you may think someone your age can't help solve them. You may think that you don't have enough money or power to make a difference. Think about the Apostles who set out with Jesus' good news. Then think about Colleen. The money she raised might help scientists find a cure for a disease.

Every time you work as the Apostles or Colleen did to make the world better, you work for the kingdom of God. Every time you feed a person who is hungry, stop a fight, or give someone hope, you are sharing the good news of Jesus.

The Catholic faith is not only about the past and the future. It is about the present. Right here, right now, you are the Church.

? What can you do right now to make the world better?

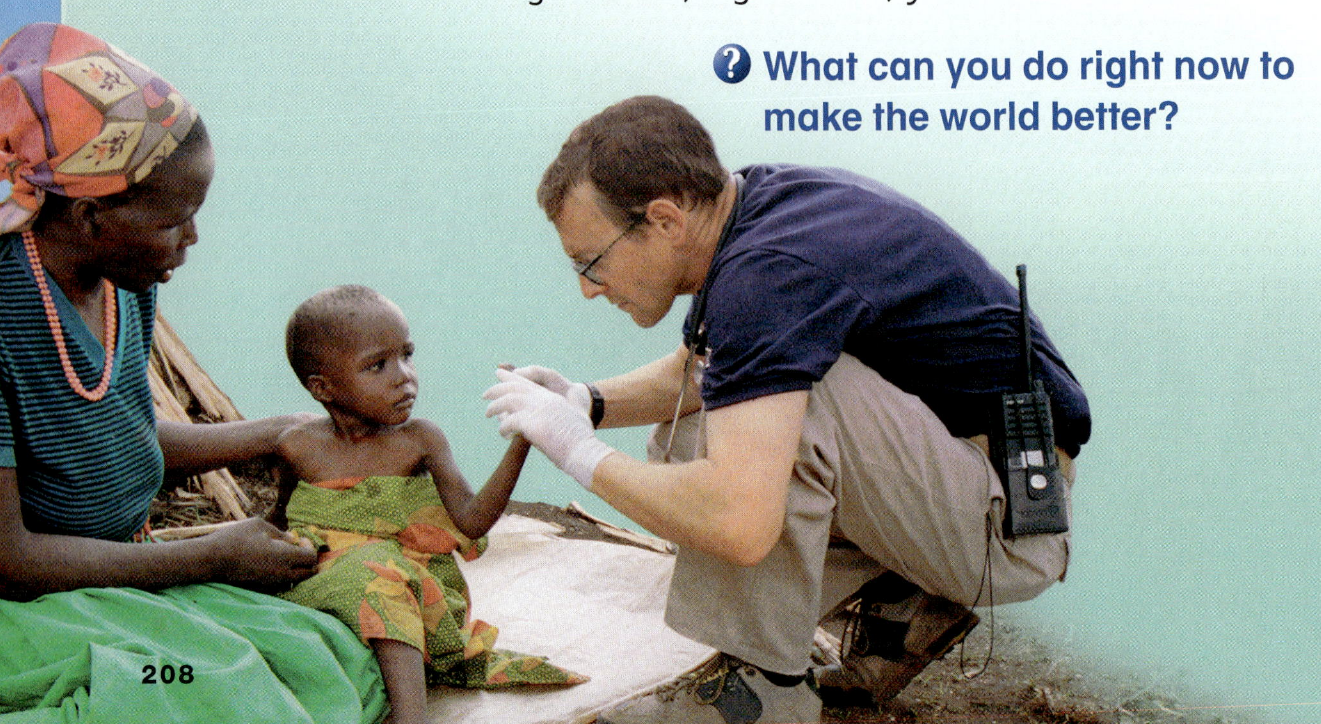

Sharing a Mission

The mission of the Church is to share the good news, to make the world holy, and to serve God and one another. The Church is a sign of God's kingdom. The Church helps people share in the love of the Holy Trinity. You do this when your words and actions show God's **justice**, love, and **peace**. You are asked to do this at your baptism.

As a member of the Church, you join in its work. The Spirit strengthens you to tell others about Jesus. You can work for everyone's basic rights, such as food, clothing, shelter, and dignity. You can care for people who are poor, ill, or lonely.

Words of Faith

Justice is the virtue of giving God and others what is their due.

Peace is the true unity among people that makes them want to respect one another and keep order. It is the good effect of working for justice.

Why Help Others?

When you help with the Church's mission, you follow the example of Jesus. You do this because all people are your sisters and brothers. God calls all people to be united in his family and to share what they have.

Activity Connect Your Faith

Send a Message People often create T-shirts to send a special message. On the T-shirt shown here, create a message about the Church's mission.

Prayer for Peace

Gather and begin with the Sign of the Cross.

Sing together.

Make me, Lord, a means of your peace;
make me, O Lord, a means of your love.
In this world, despairing and sad, make
me a source of courage and joy.
Where there is hatred, let me bring
love, where there is harm, your pardon
to soothe. Help me bring faith where
there is but doubt, and where it is
dark, the light of your truth.

Master, grant that I may not seek
so much consolation as to console,
Understanding as to understand,
so much to be loved as rather to
love. Help me to see in giving to all
how we in turn receive from your
hand, How we are pardoned as we
forgive, and how we, in death, are
born to new life.

Bow your heads as the leader prays.

All: Amen.

Review and Apply

A Work with Words Write the letter of the correct response, and then circle True or False. Correct any false statements.

	Column 1		Column 2
______	**1.** mission	**a.**	to show by words or actions
______	**2.** witness	**b.**	a job or duty that you are sent to do
______	**3.** justice	**c.**	giving people what is their due

4. Jesus' followers carried lots of money and supplies when they went out to help others.

True False ______________________________

5. When you help others today, you share in God's kingdom on earth.

True False ______________________________

B Check Understanding What is peace?

____

Activity Live Your Faith

Draw a picture of yourself working for justice or peace.

Family Faith

Catholics Believe

- All members of the Church share in its mission to work for peace and justice.
- The Church is a sign of the kingdom of God.

SCRIPTURE

Galatians 3:27–28 tells us that all people belong to Christ.

GO online **www.osvcurriculum.com** For weekly scripture readings and seasonal resources

Activity

Live Your Faith

Concern for Others Christians work to make sure that every person's human rights are protected, especially the rights of people who are poor, ill, or lonely. Create a note card that shows one way that you can help a person who is poor, ill, or lonely.

People of Faith

▲ Jean Donovan 1953–1980

Jean Donovan worked as a lay missionary in El Salvador. She shared her gifts of laughter, music, and love with children who were poor. She gave them hope. Jean was killed along with three religious sisters by the El Salvador national guard. Members of that organization feared that the four women would teach the people of El Salvador about human rights.

Family Prayer

Dear God, help us bring joy and hope to those in need. Amen.

In Unit 7 your child is learning about the KINGDOM OF GOD.

CCC *See Catechism of the Catholic Church 2044-2046 for further reading on chapter content.*

Chapter 21

Live Forever!

Leader: Loving Father, we praise your name forever.
"Your reign is a reign for all ages,
your dominion for all generations."
Psalm 145:13

All: Loving Father, we praise your name forever. Amen.

Activity Let's Begin

The Gift of Life "Grandma, what is Dad doing?" Tommy asked.

"He's bringing in all the gifts for your new baby sister," Grandma said.

Dad came in carrying flowers, balloons, and a large teddy bear. "Dad, where is Mom?" Tommy wondered.

Dad replied, "She is bringing in the most important gift, your baby sister!"

"Wow! I can't wait to see her," Tommy said, smiling.

- Have you ever welcomed a new family member? Tell about it.

Cycles of Life

What happens after death?

The cycle of life begins with birth and ends in death. Read this story about the cycle of life and dealing with loss.

A STORY

The Little Daisy

Early one spring, a little bud named Daisy grew from a seed. She became friends with a bud named Sunflower.

Daisy grew into a small white flower with a little yellow head. Sunflower grew very tall with yellow petals and a large brown head. They both loved the fresh morning dew and the warm summer sun.

One day the wind got very cold. Daisy noticed that ice had formed on her leaves.

"What is happening?" she asked.

Sunflower said, "At the end of summer, it is time for us to die. When you die, your seeds will fall back into the ground. New flowers will bloom from your seeds!"

"I feel much better now," said Daisy.

She laid her head down and said, "I've had a beautiful life."

Why did Daisy feel better after learning that flowers would bloom from her seeds?

New Life

When Jesus came to earth, he told people that if they believed in him, they would have everlasting life. His own Resurrection is the proof that his promise is true. His followers saw him alive after he had died. Later, John, who was one of Jesus' followers, had a vision from God of what would come at the end of time. This is what John said about his vision.

SCRIPTURE

I saw a new heaven and a new earth. The old creation had passed away. I saw a holy city coming out of the sky. It was like a new Jerusalem. I heard God's voice saying that there would be no more tears or sadness, no more suffering or death.

Based on *Revelation 21:1–4*

Activity Share Your Faith

Think: Imagine what a new heaven and earth would be like.

Share: What will the new heaven and earth look like? Draw a picture.

Act: Take the picture home and hang it for all to see. This will remind you of the hope that Christians have because of Jesus.

Explore

The Church's Future

What do Christians believe about the future?

The Church looks forward to a reunion with God. The Church looks beyond death to the coming of God's kingdom in its fullness.

When we die we will be judged and go to **heaven**, **hell**, or **purgatory**. At the end of time all people will be judged, as Jesus said. Those who have loved God and have loved others will live with God forever.

Just as you look forward to good times on earth, you can look forward to Christ's second coming and the **last judgment** at the end of time. Catholics live in hope that God's grace and their loving actions will lead to everlasting life with God.

Why do Christians look forward to the second coming of Christ?

The Beginning and the End

The Bible begins and ends with stories of creation. In the Book of Genesis, the first book of the Bible, you read how God created all things out of love. The last book, the Book of Revelation, ends with John's vision of a new creation. This is God's everlasting kingdom. The world and the Church will then be perfect. All faithful people will be raised to new life.

The Son of God, the Word of God, was present at the creation, and he will be present at the end of time. In John's vision Jesus Christ says,

SCRIPTURE

"I am the Alpha and the Omega, the first and the last, the beginning and the end."

Revelation 22:13

Words of Faith

Heaven is being with God forever in happiness.

Hell is being separated forever from God because of a choice to turn away from him completely.

Purgatory is a state of final cleansing before entrance into heaven.

Last judgment is at the end of time. Jesus will come again to judge the living and the dead and to bring the kingdom of God to its fullness.

Activity Connect Your Faith

Make a Bumper Sticker All people who love God and others will be with God forever. Think about a message to share with those who do not know God's love. In the box below, write a bumper sticker to share your message. Decorate your bumper sticker.

Prayer for the Kingdom

Gather and begin with the Sign of the Cross.

Leader: We gather and share a prayer for the coming of the kingdom.

Reader 1: God, we have learned so much about you this year.

Reader 2: We have taught one another about your love.

Reader 3: Help us learn even more about you in school, at home, and at play.

Reader 1: Help us grow to be more caring people, who will show your love to all who know us.

Reader 2: When our earthly lives end, judge us by our loving deeds.

Reader 3: We hope to join your saints and rejoice in your presence forever.

All: **Come, Lord Jesus! Amen.**

Sing together.

Come! Live in the
light! Shine with
the joy and the love
of the Lord! We are
called to be light for the
kingdom, to live in the
freedom of the city of God!

Review and Apply

A Check Understanding Complete each sentence with the correct term from the Word Bank.

1. Our earthly life will end in death.
2. Each peron will be judged and sent to heaven, hell, or purgatory.
3. At the end of time, Jesus will come again.
4. This is the last judgment and the second coming.
5. If you have lived with Love, you will have a place in God's kingdom forever.

WORD BANK

heaven
death
Jesus
love
last judgment
God's kingdom
hell
purgatory
judged
coming

B Make Connections Imagine that you must explain heaven to a younger child. What will you say?

____

____

Activity Live Your Faith

Remind Yourself Making loving choices and following Jesus are things you can do so that you will be part of God's kingdom forever. Make a sign that will remind you to do this over the summer.

Family Faith

Catholics Believe

- People who die in God's friendship live forever in God's presence.
- At the end of the world, Christ will judge all people on the way they lived their lives.

SCRIPTURE

John 14:1–4 is about Jesus' preparing a place for you. Read the verses and talk about them with your family.

GO online **www.osvcurriculum.com**
For weekly scripture readings and seasonal resources

Activity

Live Your Faith

Family Project Have a special family gathering for remembering loved ones who have died. Tell stories about how those people showed love. Pray that they find joy and peace in God's kingdom.

People of Faith

Dismas was one of the two criminals who were crucified at the same time as Jesus. Dismas admitted his own guilt and said that he deserved punishment for his actions. Then Dismas said, "Jesus, remember me when you come into your kingdom" *(Luke 23:42)*. Jesus replied that Dismas would be in paradise with him that same day.

▲ **Saint Dismas died c. A.D. 33**

Family Prayer

Saint Dismas, pray for us that we may see things as clearly as you did. Help us be close to Jesus now and at the hour of our death. Amen.

In Unit 7 your child is learning about the KINGDOM OF GOD.

CCC *See Catechism of the Catholic Church 1023–1029, 1039 for further reading on chapter content.*

Unit 7 Review

A Work with Words Circle the letter of the choice that best completes each sentence.

1. A ______ is a sacred promise between God and humans.
   - a. vow
   - b. covenant
   - c. commitment
2. ______ is the state of preparation before heaven.
   - a. purification
   - b. hell
   - c. purgatory
3. ______ is being separated from God forever.
   - a. purgatory
   - b. hell
   - c. darkness
4. ______ is the virtue that moves people to give God and their neighbors what is their due.
   - a. peace
   - b. charity
   - c. justice
5. ______ is being with God forever.
   - a. peace
   - b. justice
   - c. heaven

B Check Understanding Complete each sentence with the correct word(s) from the Word Bank.

WORD BANK

last judgment
Israel
witness
death
peace

6. Abraham's family grew to become the people of ____________.
7. To show by words or action is to ____________.
8. ____________ makes people want to respect one another.
9. Our earthly lives will end in ____________.
10. At the ________________________, Jesus will come to judge the living and the dead.

Catholic Source Book

Scripture

The Bible

The **Bible** is a holy book. The Bible is also called Scripture. It contains God's word written down by humans. The Bible is made up of two parts, the Old Testament and the New Testament. Many different books are included in the Bible.

Faith Fact

Jewish people call the first five books of their Bible the *Torah*.

Old Testament

The Old Testament is also called the Hebrew Scriptures. It tells the story of the Hebrew people and their covenant with God. The Church reads from the Old Testament at most Masses. The Old Testament includes Bible stories that you know. The stories of Adam and Eve, Noah, Abraham and Sarah, Moses, Joseph and his brothers, and King David are in the Old Testament. These stories tell you about your ancestors in faith.

New Testament

The New Testament tells the story of our faith since Jesus was born. The first four books are called the Gospels. They tell about Jesus' life on earth and how he died and rose to save us. A book called the *Acts of the Apostles* tells how the Church grew after Jesus returned to his Father. Letters from Saint Paul and other Church leaders tell Jesus' followers how to live their faith. Finally, the Book of Revelation encouraged Christians who were being persecuted, and, in some ways, tells what will happen at the end of time, when Jesus comes again in glory.

Gospels

The word *gospel* means "good news." The gospel message is the good news of God's kingdom and saving love. The Church gives the name *Gospels* to the first four books of the New Testament that tell about Jesus' life and teachings. Every Mass includes a reading from one of the four Gospels.

Parables

Parables are teaching stories. Jesus used parables to tell about the kingdom of God. Parables also tell how to live in the kingdom. The story of the Pharisee and the tax collector is a parable. It teaches about the right way to pray.

The Kingdom of God

The kingdom of God means two things. The kingdom of God is here on earth right now. It happens when Jesus' followers share the good news and show God's love and care to others. The kingdom of God will come in fullness at the end of time. Then Jesus' followers will live forever with God in perfect peace and joy.

Letters

Saint Paul made visits to churches in distant places. He helped the churches grow and spread the good news. He also wrote letters to the churches he visited. He gave advice on how to solve problems and how to work together as Jesus' followers. These letters are part of the New Testament. One reading at Mass comes from a letter of Saint Paul or another early Church leader.

Bible Verses

To learn how to read Bible citations, use the example of *Matthew 8:23–27*.

Matthew is the name of a book in the Bible. The chapter number always comes after the name of the book, so 8 is the chapter number. The numbers 23–27 are line numbers.

God

There are three Persons in one God—God the Father, God the Son, and God the Holy Spirit. The word for three Persons in one God is **Trinity**.

God the Father

Christians honor God the Father as the creator of all that exists. The Church prays to God the Father. Jesus taught his followers that God was his Father and their Father, too. Jesus said to pray using the words, "Our Father, who art in heaven."

God the Son

Christians honor Jesus, God the Son, as the Savior of all people. Jesus is God, and he also became human.

Christians believe that Jesus is the Messiah, God's chosen one. *Messiah* is a Hebrew word that means "the anointed one" or "the one chosen by God." Jesus was chosen to save humans from sin and death.

God the Holy Spirit

Christians honor God the Holy Spirit as the person who helps and guides us. The Holy Spirit supports and comforts us and helps us live holier lives. The Church uses symbols to describe the Holy Spirit. A dove, a flame, and the wind are all symbols of the Holy Spirit.

New Testament Names

Some people are never called by name in the New Testament. Over time, the Church has given them names. Among these traditional names are Casper, Melchior, and Balthasar for the three wise men who brought gifts to the Christ Child.

The Church

The Church is the community of all baptized people who believe in God and follow Jesus. The word *church* comes from two different words. One means "a community called together." The other means "belonging to the Lord." The Church is also sometimes called the "People of God."

Another name for the Church is "The Body of Christ." This name shows that you are closely joined with others and with Jesus. Church members work together just as parts of the body work together. The Church's mission is to tell the good news of God's kingdom.

Faith Fact

Popes' Names

Each newly elected pope chooses a name for himself. The chosen name usually honors a holy person the new pope admires. But out of respect, no new pope has called himself Peter II.

The Communion of Saints

All people living and dead who believe in Jesus and follow his way are part of the communion of saints. This includes people now alive on earth and people who have died and are now in purgatory or heaven. People on earth join in the communion of saints when they celebrate the Eucharist.

Church Leaders

The pope, cardinals, bishops and archbishops, pastors, and other priests lead and guide Jesus' followers. This chart shows how the Church's leaders are organized.

Marks of the Church

There are four marks of the Church. We say the Church is one, holy, catholic, and apostolic.

1. The Church is **one** because the power of the Holy Spirit unites all the members in one faith.
2. The Church is **holy** because it shows God's holiness.
3. The Church is **catholic** because Jesus sent the Church out to tell the good news to the whole world.
4. The Church is **apostolic** because the Apostles worked with Jesus to begin the Church. The Church today teaches what the Apostles taught, and the bishops lead in the place of the Apostles.

The Twelve Apostles

Peter
James
John
Andrew
Philip
Thomas
Bartholomew
Matthew
James, son of Alphaeus
Simon the Zealot
Judas
Matthias

Life After Death

The Church looks forward to the coming of God's kingdom. When a Christian dies, he or she looks forward to the promise of life forever with God.

Faith Fact

Which Way?

Churches in Europe were usually built facing east, so that the morning sun would shine on the altar. A church that faced east would also be pointing toward the holy city of Jerusalem.

Heaven, Hell, and Purgatory

After people die, they will be in heaven, hell, or purgatory. Heaven is being happy with God forever. Hell is being separated from God forever. Purgatory is a preparation for heaven after death. The word *purgatory* means "making pure." Purgatory makes a person ready to be with God in heaven.

Judgment

At the end of time, all Christians look forward to a time of happiness and peace. At that time Jesus will come again to judge the living and the dead. Then the kingdom of God will come in fullness. The Church calls these events the second coming and the last judgment. These are times of hope and joy for Christians. Jesus' followers believe in the promise of God's everlasting kingdom.

Mary

Mary is Jesus' mother. For this reason she is called the Mother of God. The Church honors Mary because she was willing to do what God asked. Mary is a model for Christians of all times and places.

Titles of Mary

The Church honors Mary with many titles. Each tells something about her and why she is so loved. Mary is called the Immaculate Conception, the Blessed Virgin, the Madonna, Our Lady of Perpetual Help, Queen of Heaven, Help of Christians, the Morning Star, and Queen of Angels.

Mary Names

Many Christians honor Mary by naming their children after her. Mary, Marie, and Maria are forms of the name you may know. Marilyn, Maureen, Moira, Marianne, and Marita are names that mean "Mary" in other languages. The name *Madonna* means "my lady" in Italian. *Regina* means "queen" in Latin. And Virginia is a name that refers to Mary's virginity. In Spanish-speaking countries children are also named Lupe (for Our Lady of Guadalupe), Concepción (for the Immaculate Conception), Dolores (for Our Lady of Sorrows), or Gracia (for Our Lady of Grace). Fatima and Lourdes, places where Mary has appeared, have also been used as names to honor the Mother of God.

Liturgy

The Mass

The Mass includes two main parts: the Liturgy of the Word and the Liturgy of the Eucharist. At the Liturgy of the Word you listen to the word of God. There are readings from Scripture. The priest gives a homily. He explains the readings and tells Christians how to carry out the Church's mission.

The Liturgy of the Eucharist includes prayers and songs thanking and praising God, and offering the gifts of bread and wine. Then the priest blesses the bread and wine, which become the Body and Blood of Christ. Church members give one another a sign of peace. This shows they are ready to come to the Lord's table. The people share in Jesus' sacrifice when they receive Communion.

When the Mass ends, Church members are sent to "Go and announce the Gospel of the Lord" in their own community.

Faith Fact

Native American Masses

The Mass has been translated into two Native American languages, Navajo and Choctaw.

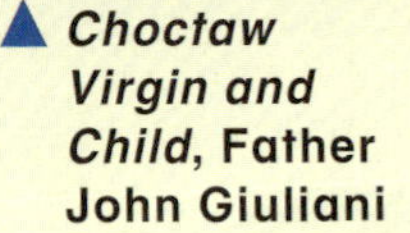

▲ ***Choctaw Virgin and Child*, Father John Giuliani**

Order of Mass

The Mass follows a pattern, with some differences according to the feast or season of the liturgical year. The main parts of the Mass are the Liturgy of the Word and the Liturgy of the Eucharist. Here is an outline of the Order of Mass:

Introductory Rites

- Entrance Chant
- Greeting
- Rite for the Blessing and Sprinkling of Water
- Penitential Act
- Kyrie
- Gloria
- Collect

Liturgy of the Word

- First Reading
- Responsorial Psalm
- Second Reading
- Gospel Acclamation
- Dialogue at the Gospel
- Gospel Reading
- Homily
- Profession of Faith
- Prayer of the Faithful

Liturgy of the Eucharist

- Preparation of the Gifts
- Invitation to Prayer
- Prayer over the Offerings
- Eucharistic Prayer
  - Preface Dialogue
  - Preface
  - Preface Acclamation
  - Consecration
  - Mystery of Faith
  - Concluding Doxology
- Communion Rite
  - The Lord's Prayer
  - Sign of Peace
  - Lamb of God (*Agnus Dei*)
  - Invitation to Communion
  - Communion
  - Prayer after Communion

Concluding Rites

- Greeting
- Blessing
- Dismissal

The Sacraments

Sacraments of Initiation

Baptism
Confirmation
Eucharist

Sacraments of Healing

Reconciliation
Anointing of the Sick

Sacraments of Service

Matrimony
Holy Orders

Sacramentals

Sacramentals remind you of God. Sacramentals often include an action like the Sign of the Cross. Crucifixes, holy cards, and medals remind you of Jesus, the Blessed Mother, or the saints. Palm branches remind you of Jesus' entry into Jerusalem. After the Palm Sunday service, you can keep and display the palm branches in your home. These are all popular sacramentals.

Blessings

A blessing is a special sign and prayer. Blessings praise God. They ask for God's care for a person, a place, a thing, or an action. In many churches on the feast day of Saint Francis of Assisi (October 4), the priest blesses pets or farm animals.

Devotions

Devotions are special prayers that honor God, Mary, or the saints. Visits to the Blessed Sacrament are a popular devotion to honor Jesus. The Rosary is a devotion to honor Mary. Devotions help people remember to pray outside of the Mass.

Sacred Places

A *cathedral* is the home church of a diocese. It is in the city where the bishop or archbishop leads his people. A *basilica* is a church given special importance by the pope. Catholics make pilgrimages, or special visits, to basilicas.

Objects in the Church Building

- **altar** The altar is the central table in the front of the church. The priest celebrates Mass at the altar.
- **Paschal candle** A large, decorated candle lit from the new fire at the Easter Vigil. This candle is lit at all the Masses during the Easter Season. It is also lit at baptisms and funerals.
- **ambo** A place where Scripture is read and homilies are preached. The ambo is also called the pulpit or lectern.
- **tabernacle** A place to keep and worship the Blessed Sacrament.

- **baptismal font or pool** The container that holds the water for Baptism.

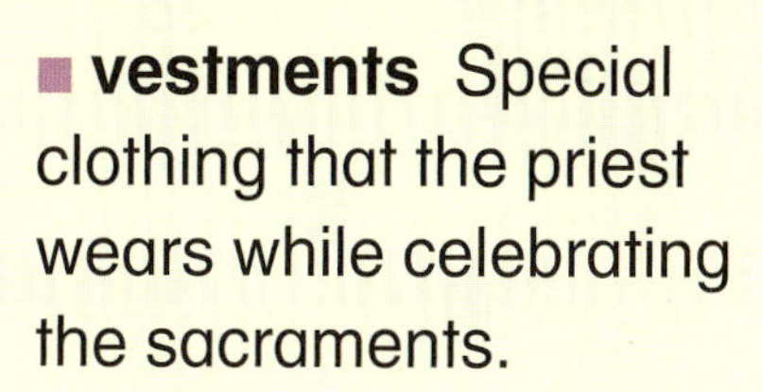

- **vestments** Special clothing that the priest wears while celebrating the sacraments.

Liturgical Colors

Certain colors are used during certain seasons of the Church year. These colors are used for parts of the priest's vestments.

Green: Sundays in Ordinary Time

Red: Palm Sunday, Good Friday, Pentecost

Rose: Third Sunday of Advent and Fourth Sunday of Lent

Purple or **Violet:** Advent and Lent

White: Christmas, Easter, Feasts of the Lord, Mary, and the saints not martyred, or funerals

The Ten Commandments

The Ten Commandments	Their Meaning
1. I am the LORD your God: You shall not have strange Gods before me.	Keep God first in your life.
2. You shall not take the name of the LORD your God in vain.	Always use God's name in a reverent way.
3. Remember to keep holy the LORD's day.	Attend Mass and rest on Sunday.
4. Honor your father and your mother.	Obey your parents and guardians.
5. You shall not kill.	Care for yourself and others.
6. You shall not commit adultery.	Be respectful of every person.
7. You shall not steal.	Respect other people and their property.
8. You shall not bear false witness against your neighbor.	Respect others by always telling the truth.
9. You shall not covet your neighbor's wife.	Don't be jealous of other people's friendships.
10. You shall not covet your neighbor's goods.	Don't be jealous of what other people have.

The Great Commandment

[Jesus] said in reply, "You shall love the Lord your God with all your heart, with all your soul, with all your strength, with all your mind; and your neighbor as yourself."

Luke 10:27

The Beatitudes

Blessed are the poor in spirit,
for theirs is the kingdom of heaven.
Blessed are they who mourn,
for they will be comforted.
Blessed are the meek,
for they will inherit the land.
Blessed are they who hunger and thirst for
righteousness,
for they will be satisfied.
Blessed are the merciful,
for they will be shown mercy.
Blessed are the clean of heart,
for they will see God.
Blessed are the peacemakers,
for they will be called children of God.
Blessed are they who are persecuted for the
sake of righteousness,
for theirs is the kingdom of heaven.

Matthew 5:3–10

Lady Wisdom

Parts of the Old Testament speak of wisdom as a person, usually a woman. The name Sophia comes from the Greek word for wisdom.

Morality

Examination of Conscience

1. Pray to the Holy Spirit to help you examine your conscience.
2. Read the Beatitudes, the Ten Commandments, the Great Commandment, and the precepts of the Church.
3. Ask yourself these questions:

   When have I not done what God wants me to do?
   Whom have I hurt?
   What have I done that I knew was wrong?
   What have I not done that I should have done?
   Have I done penance and tried to change?
   With what am I still having trouble?
   Am I sorry for all my sins?

Grace

Grace is God's life in you. Grace is not something physical. You receive the gift of grace in a special way at Baptism. You grow in God's grace through celebrating the sacraments.

Solidarity

All people, especially those in need, are your sisters and brothers. When people are united in God's family, and when they share joys and sorrows with others, they are in solidarity with one another.

Virtue

Making good and loving choices helps you develop habits of goodness, called virtues. The word *virtue* means "strength." Practicing these habits of goodness helps you to make even more loving choices. The *theological virtues* of faith, hope, and love are gifts from God.

Faith—Faith is believing in God and all that God has shown you. You believe because Jesus taught you how to live.

Hope—Hope is the virtue that helps you trust in what God has shown you. It is the gift of looking forward to the happiness of life forever with God and the coming of God's kingdom.

Love—You show your love for God by praising God and loving other people. You help people. You listen to friends who have problems. You do kind things. The Church wants you to show love for God by treating everyone with kindness and respect.

Names and Titles for Jesus

Jesus has been given many names and titles. Each tells something special about Jesus or is a way to honor him. These names and titles include Christ, Savior, Lord, Lamb of God (*Agnus Dei*), Son of God, Son of Man, the Word, and the Suffering Servant.

Prayer

The Sign of the Cross

In the name of the Father, and of the Son,
  and of the Holy Spirit.
Amen.

The Lord's Prayer

Our Father,
  who art in heaven,
hallowed be thy name;
thy kingdom come,
thy will be done
  on earth as it is in heaven.
Give us this day our daily bread,
and forgive us our trespasses
as we forgive those who
  trespass against us;
and lead us not into temptation,
but deliver us from evil.
Amen.

Hail Mary

Hail, Mary, full of grace,
the Lord is with you!
Blessed are you among women,
and blessed is the fruit of your womb, Jesus.
Holy Mary, Mother of God,
pray for us sinners,
now and at the hour of our death.
Amen.

Glory to the Father (Doxology)

Glory to the Father, and to the Son, and to the Holy Spirit:
as it was in the beginning, is now, and will be for ever.
Amen.

Blessing Before Meals

Bless us, O Lord, and these your gifts
which we are about to receive from your goodness.
Through Christ our Lord.
Amen.

Thanksgiving After Meals

We give you thanks for all your gifts, almighty God, living and reigning now and for ever.
Amen.

Act of Faith, Hope, and Love

My God, I believe in you,
I trust in you,
I love you above all things,
with all my heart and mind and strength.
I love you because you are supremely good and worth loving;
and because I love you,
I am sorry with all my heart for offending you.
Lord, have mercy on me, a sinner.
Amen.

Faith Fact

A Longer Lord's Prayer

Many Christians include an extra line at the end of the Lord's Prayer: "The kingdom, and the power, and the glory are yours, now and forever."

Prayer to the Holy Spirit

Come, Holy Spirit, fill the hearts of your faithful.
And kindle in them the fire of your love.
Send forth your Spirit and they shall be created.
And you will renew the face of the earth.

The Apostles' Creed

I believe in God,
the Father almighty,
Creator of heaven and earth,
and in Jesus Christ, his only Son, our Lord,

At the words that follow, up to and including the Virgin Mary, *all bow.*

who was conceived by the Holy Spirit,
born of the Virgin Mary,
suffered under Pontius Pilate,
was crucified, died and was buried;
he descended into hell;
on the third day he rose again from the dead;
he ascended into heaven,
and is seated at the right hand of God the Father almighty;
from there he will come to judge the living and the dead.
I believe in the Holy Spirit,
the holy catholic Church,
the communion of saints,
the forgiveness of sins,
the resurrection of the body,
and life everlasting. Amen.

Act of Contrition

My God,
I am sorry for my sins with all my heart.
In choosing to do wrong
and failing to do good,
I have sinned against you
whom I should love above all things.
I firmly intend, with your help,
to do penance,
to sin no more,
and to avoid whatever leads me to sin.
Our Savior Jesus Christ
suffered and died for us.
In his name, my God, have mercy.

Amen

"Amen" is a Hebrew word that shows agreement. You say "Amen" at the end of most prayers to show that you believe the words of the prayer are true.

Prayer of Blessing for a Child's Birthday

Loving God,
you created all the people of the world
and you know each of us by name.
We thank you for N.,
who today celebrates his/her birthday.
Bless him/her with your love and friendship
that he/she may grow in wisdom, knowledge,
and grace.
May he/she love his/her family always
and be faithful to his/her friends.
Grant this through Christ our Lord.
Amen.

Book of Blessings, paragraph 336B

Morning Offering

Almighty God, we thank you
for the life and light of a new day.
Keep us safe today
and protect us from every evil.
We offer ourselves this day to you
through Jesus Christ your son.
May your Holy Spirit
make our thoughts, words, and actions
pleasing in your sight.
Amen.

Faith Fact

We begin each day and end each day with prayer. That is because we want to thank God for everything he does for us. We ask him to be with us always.

Evening Prayer

Protect us, Lord, as we stay awake;
watch over us as we sleep,
that awake, we may keep watch with Christ,
and asleep, rest in his peace.
Amen.

Grace Before Mealtime

The eyes of all look to you, O Lord,
to give them their food in due season.
You open wide your hands
and fill all things with your blessings,
through Christ our Lord.
Amen.

Grace After Mealtime

For these and his many mercies,
may the Lord's name be blessed,
now and forever,
through Christ our Lord.
Amen.

See page 239 for more mealtime prayers.

Prayer

Angel Guardian

(traditional)

Angel of God,
my guardian dear,
to whom God's love
commits me here,
ever this day (night)
be at my side,
to light and guard,
to rule and guide.
Amen.

Angel Guardian

(contemporary)

Angel sent by God to guide me,
be my light and walk beside me;
be my guardian and protect me;
on the paths of life direct me.

Angelus

V. The angel spoke God's message to Mary,
R. and she conceived of the Holy
Spirit.
Hail, Mary . . .

V. "I am the lowly servant of the Lord:
R. let it be done to me according to your word."
Hail, Mary . . .

V. And the Word became flesh,
R. and lived among us.
Hail, Mary . . .

V. Pray for us, holy Mother of God,
R. that we may become worthy of the
promises of Christ.

Let us pray.

Lord,
fill our hearts with your grace:
once, through the message of an angel
you revealed to us the incarnation of
your Son;
now, through his suffering and death
lead us to the glory of his resurrection.

We ask this through Christ our Lord.
Amen.

Faith Fact

The *Angelus* is a prayer honoring the Incarnation. It is given its name by the first word of the Latin version of the prayer: *Angelus Domini nuntiavit Maria*, "The angel of the Lord declared unto Mary." To honor the Incarnation, it is recited three times each day—morning, noon, and evening, at the sound of the *Angelus* bell. Each response, where shown, is followed by reciting the Hail Mary.

How to Pray the Rosary

1. Pray the Sign of the Cross and say the Apostles' Creed.
2. Pray the Lord's Prayer.
3. Pray three Hail Marys.
4. Pray the Glory to the Father.
5. Say the first mystery; then pray the Lord's Prayer.
6. Pray ten Hail Marys while meditating on the mystery.
7. Pray the Glory to the Father.
8. Say the second mystery; then pray the Lord's Prayer. Repeat 6 and 7 and continue with the third, fourth, and fifth mysteries in the same manner.
9. Pray the Hail, Holy Queen.

Faith Fact

As the Mother of Jesus, the Son of God, Mary is called the Mother of God, the Queen of all Saints, and the Mother of the Church. There are many prayers and practices of devotion to Mary. One of the most popular is the Rosary. It focuses on the twenty mysteries that describe the events in the lives of Jesus and Mary.

The Mysteries of the Rosary

The Joyful Mysteries	The Luminous Mysteries
The Annunciation The Visitation The Nativity The Presentation in the Temple The Finding in the Temple	The Baptism of Jesus The Wedding at Cana The Proclamation of the Kingdom The Transfiguration The Institution of the Eucharist
The Sorrowful Mysteries	**The Glorious Mysteries**
The Agony in the Garden The Scourging at the Pillar The Crowning with Thorns The Carrying of the Cross The Crucifixion and Death	The Resurrection The Ascension The Descent of the Holy Spirit The Assumption of Mary The Coronation of Mary in Heaven

Prayer of Petition

Lord God, you know our weakness.
In your mercy grant that the example
of your saints may bring us back to
love and serve you through Christ
our Lord.
Amen.

Prayer of Community Petition

God of love, our strength and
protection, hear the prayer of
your Church.
Grant that when we come to you in
faith, our prayers may be answered,
through Christ our Lord.
Amen.

Holy, Holy, Holy Lord

In English

Holy, Holy, Holy Lord God of hosts.
Heaven and earth are full of your glory.
Hosanna in the highest.
Blessed is he who comes in the name of the Lord.
Hosanna in the highest.

In Latin

Sanctus, Sanctus, Sanctus
Dominus Deus Sabaoth.
Pleni sunt coeli et terra gloria tua.
Hosanna in excelsis.

Benedictus qui venit in nomine Domini.
Hosanna in excelsis.

Lamb of God

In English

Lamb of God, you take away the
sins of the world,
have mercy on us.
Lamb of God, you take away the
sins of the world,
have mercy on us.
Lamb of God, you take away the
sins of the world,
grant us peace.

In Latin

Agnus Dei, qui tollis peccata mundi,
miserere nobis.
Agnus Dei, qui tollis peccata mundi,
miserere nobis.
Agnus Dei, qui tollis peccata mundi,
dona nobis pacem.

Faith Fact

As members of the Catholic Church, we usually pray in the language that we speak, but we sometimes pray in Latin, the common language of the Church. The following are a couple of the common prayers of the Church in both English and Latin.

Faith in Action!
CATHOLIC SOCIAL TEACHING

DISCOVER

Catholic Social Teaching:

Care for God's Creation

Care for Creation

When you show God that you are grateful for creation, you are a good steward, or caregiver, of creation. Here are some ways to show you care.

- **Be grateful for foods that come from the earth.** Apples, berries, corn, and other fruits and vegetables are gifts from the earth that help keep people healthy.
- **Care for other people.** People are the most important part of creation.
- **Use natural resources with care.** The water you drink, the air you breathe, and the land used to grow food are needed for all life on earth. Taking care of them and using them well show that you are a good steward.

How do you already care for creation?

CONNECT

With the Call to Justice

Buy Our Vegetables!

God asks you to care for all of his creation. Let's see how one parish shows that it cares.

At St. Joan of Arc Catholic Church in Minnesota, parishioners grow vegetables in a special garden. But they don't eat a single pepper, pumpkin, or ear of corn! They sell the food they raise to earn money for the needs of the community.

St. Joan's Farmer's Market started with the idea of raising food on the church's property. A sunny location was chosen. Then parishioners traded with local residents for fertilizer, seeds, and plants. Volunteers came every week to care for the crops. When harvest time came, the Farmer's Market was ready to open.

All of the money raised at the Farmer's Market is given to help others. One year St. Joan's raised $761.63 for Second Harvest, a group that gives food to homeless shelters, food pantries, and soup kitchens. The parishioners of St. Joan's make good use of the earth and help their neighbors in need. They are an example of good stewards of creation!

What lessons about caring for creation did the parishioners of St. Joan's learn?

SERVE

Your Community

Reach Out!

Show Thanks and Care

Planting a garden and caring for it is one way you can show God that you are thankful for the wonderful world he created. Think of some other ways that you and your classmates can care for God's creation, and then write your ideas on the flower.

Make a Difference

Creation in Your Community There are many creation projects that you and your classmates can participate in, such as growing trees from seeds or seedlings and sharing the young trees with neighbors or local organizations. This will make your community more beautiful and help create more oxygen for all community residents.

DISCOVER

Catholic Social Teaching:

Life and Dignity of the Human Person

Life and Dignity

At times, you might be tempted to think that people's value comes from how much money they have or the nice clothes they wear. When you think that, you are seeing as the world sees. God calls you to see as he sees!

When you see as God sees, you know that every human is a beloved child of God. Even when a person's actions make it hard to see God's goodness in him or her, the person is still created in God's image and is loved by God. Every Catholic is called by faith to respect all persons and to see the value in their lives

How can you treat everyone you meet with dignity and respect?

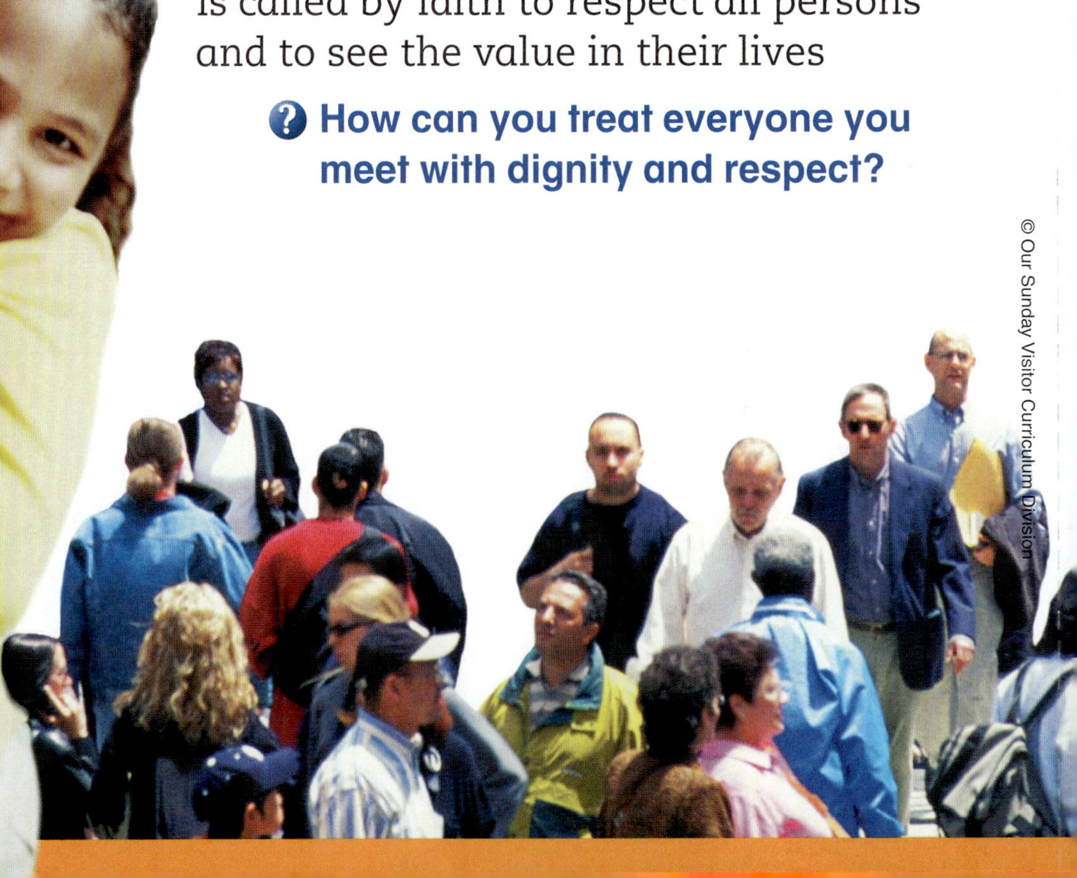

CONNECT

With the Call to Justice

Be Well!

God calls you to treat one another with love and dignity. Let's look at what one community did to show God's love.

The parishioners of St. Joseph Church in a town in Louisiana wanted to help people in their area. Many of the homeless people in town had no medical care and no money to buy medicine. The church members decided to open a Wellness Center.

Two religious orders of priests and religious brothers and sisters gave money to the parish. Parish members turned an unused room in the church into the Wellness Center. At the center, homeless people are welcome to come for medical care and medicine. They can also learn more about how to stay healthy.

When people come to the Wellness Center, they are always treated with dignity and respect. They are made to feel at home by the volunteers, who provide hospitality, coffee, and cookies as well as health care

What do you think is the most important thing that is done for the people who visit the Wellness Center?

Reach Out!

Share Life and Respect

God wants you to treat everyone fairly and with respect. He also wants all people to live happy, healthy lives. Place a heart ♥ next to the things that are needed for life. Place a star ★ next to things you can do to show respect for other people.

Life

_____ enough food

_____ lots of candy and treats

_____ warm clothing

_____ a place to live

_____ a sports car

_____ good health

_____ a swimming pool

Respect

_____ ignore people you don't like

_____ be friendly and polite

_____ share what you have

_____ laugh at people who are different

_____ call people by name

_____ ask questions and listen to answers

Make a Difference

Show You Care Together with your classmates, prepare bags of healthful snacks or personal hygiene articles, such as toothpaste and shaving cream, to donate to a local soup kitchen or shelter. The supplies for the bags might be donated by your families or by local businesses.

DISCOVER

Catholic Social Teaching:

Rights and Responsibilities of the Human Person

Rights and Responsibilities

Every person has human rights. These are the basic things that are needed for people to live happy, healthy lives in freedom and peace, according to God's plan. All people should have a safe place to live, clean water to drink, and enough food to eat. Everyone should be free to worship. All people should be treated fairly.

Education is a human right.

As followers of Jesus, Christians have a special responsibility. One of the most important jobs is helping when someone's human rights have been taken away. When Christians help protect the rights of others, they are doing the work of Jesus.

Why are Christians responsible for the human rights of others?

CONNECT

With the Call to Justice

Down on the Farm

All people have rights as humans. Let's look at a group that is working to share God's love by providing for people's basic human rights.

Nazareth Farm doesn't have cows, chickens, horses, or sheep. Nazareth Farm has a group of Christians who want their neighbors to enjoy their human rights.

Nazareth Farm in West Virginia is beautiful, with clean air and water and wonderful mountains and forests. But many people who live nearby need new homes or repairs to old homes. By helping build and repair homes, members of Nazareth Farm help provide decent housing, a basic human right.

Members of Nazareth Farm also tutor children and spend time with the elderly. Most of all, they share their friendship and love with their neighbors. Every summer thousands of teenage volunteers come to help. Their hard work and the love they give to and receive from their West Virginia neighbors show that they are truly followers of Jesus.

What lessons do you think the volunteers of Nazareth Farm learn every day?

WELCOME TO NAZARETH FARM

Volunteers improve housing.

Nazareth Farm's workers

Reach Out!

Show That You Are Jesus' Friend

The friends and followers of Jesus are called to live as Jesus lived. Jesus showed you how to care for others. When you live as Jesus lived, you are acting with justice, forgiveness, and love.

How can you make the world more just and fair?

____

____

How can you bring more forgiveness to your family and friends?

____

____

How can you act with love so that people will know you as a friend of Jesus?

____

____

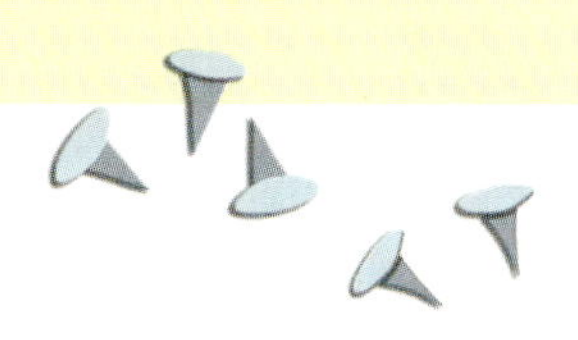

Make a Difference

Share the Message Put on a skit about human rights. Tell about how one person or a group of people do not have one of the human rights. Also show how one Christian or a group of Christians might make the situation better. Perform your skit for another class, for your families, or for a school assembly.

DISCOVER

Catholic Social Teaching:

The Dignity of Work and the Rights of Workers

The Dignity of Work

Work is not just a way to make money. Through work each day, humans join in God's work of creation. All work and all workers have dignity and value.

Workers are not always treated with the dignity and respect they deserve. Some workers earn too little pay and work too many hours. Others work in places that are not safe.

The Catholic Church wants all workers to be treated with respect and dignity. All workers must earn enough money to take care of their families. All workers should be able to work in safe places.

How can you appreciate the work your family does?

CONNECT

With the Call to Justice

Who Needs Work?

God calls people to work for many reasons. Find out what one parish is doing to help workers in their area.

Saint James the Apostle Catholic Church in Illinois is a busy parish, but parishioners there are always willing to do more. They decided to help local people find jobs with dignity, and paychecks that would support their families.

They began an employment ministry called Saint Joseph the Worker Ministry. The ministry is named for the foster father of Jesus. Saint Joseph was a carpenter. He is the patron saint of workers and all those looking for good jobs.

The Saint Joseph Ministry offers people advice in getting good jobs or changing to better jobs. Volunteers can help a person write a resumé that tells why he or she would be good at a particular job. They help job seekers plan for interviews. The ministry also provides spiritual support so that the job seekers don't lose hope or courage.

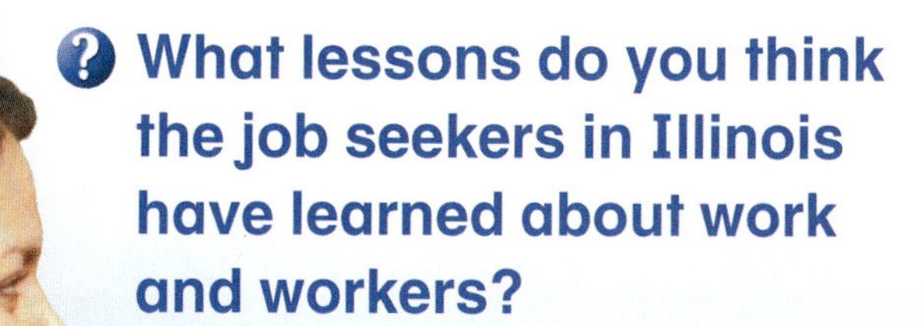

What lessons do you think the job seekers in Illinois have learned about work and workers?

SERVE

Your Community

Reach Out!

Value Your Own Work

Your classroom is a workplace, too. Doing your best work joins your work with God's work of creation.

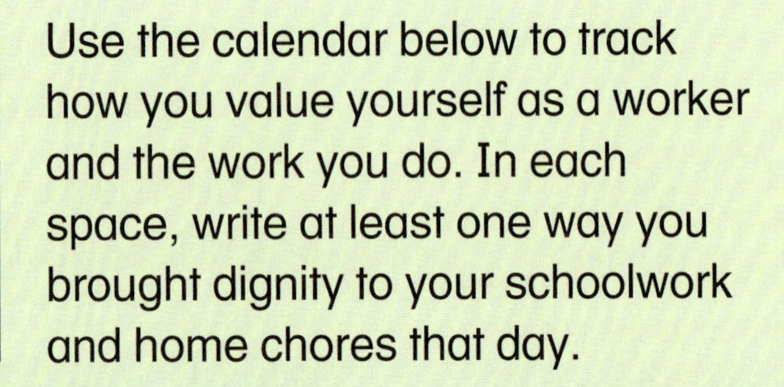

Use the calendar below to track how you value yourself as a worker and the work you do. In each space, write at least one way you brought dignity to your schoolwork and home chores that day.

My Work Has Dignity

Monday	Tuesday	Wednesday	Thursday	Friday

Make a Difference

Gather Information Interview an adult you know and ask about his or her job. Ask whether the job pays enough so that workers can afford what their families need. Ask whether the person feels respected for the work he or she does. Work with classmates to create a report called "Work and Workers in Our Area."

Write one thing you learned from working on this report:

____

Work and Workers in Our Area

DISCOVER

Catholic Social Teaching:

Solidarity of the Human Family

Solidarity

Have you ever wondered how many people are in the human family? About six and a half billion people live on earth today. All of those people are brothers and sisters in the family of God. When your brothers and sisters anywhere on earth have troubles, you should find ways to help them. Taking care of everyone in the world shows solidarity, which means friendship and unity with everyone God created.

You show solidarity when you help bring peace to others. Sometimes you work for peace in your own family and neighborhood. Sometimes you need to help people who live far away. Wherever help is needed, Jesus calls his followers to bring his peace.

? How can you be a person of peace every day?

CONNECT

With the Call to Justice

Peace Through Song

God calls you to help people around the world. Let's see how some choir members helped their brothers and sisters in a place far from home.

All Saints Catholic Church in Wisconsin has parishioners who come from Uganda in central Africa. Uganda has long suffered from war, violence, and poverty.

All Saints parishioners "adopted" a sister parish in Uganda called Our Lady of Fatima. Our Lady of Fatima adopted All Saints, too. Both parishes learned that they had something in common—their love of singing.

Soon the parish choir from Wisconsin planned a trip through Uganda. At each town, the choir sang, prayed, and shared laughter with the Ugandan people. The Ugandans offered the Americans hospitality, faith, and joy.

After returning home, the All Saints choir members were still filled with the peace and joy of Jesus. Friendship and love of music helped people from two different lands discover that they are not so different.

? What lessons might the people of Wisconsin have learned from the people of Uganda?

Reach Out!

SERVE

Your Community

Discover the World

You may not be able to travel to Uganda, but you can learn about people around the world with whom you would like to share friendship and solidarity. Many books tell about people and life in other places. Discover the names and authors of three such books and write them here.

____

____

____

Combine your list with those of your classmates to make a Friends Around the World Reading List. Read at least a few of these books during the school year or over the summer.

Make a Difference

Make Friends Pen pal organizations help children and adults find the names and addresses of people living in this country and in other countries. See whether you can find such an organization and get involved. For now, write a letter that could introduce you to someone your age from another country or culture. Include a message of peace or God's love that you would like to share.

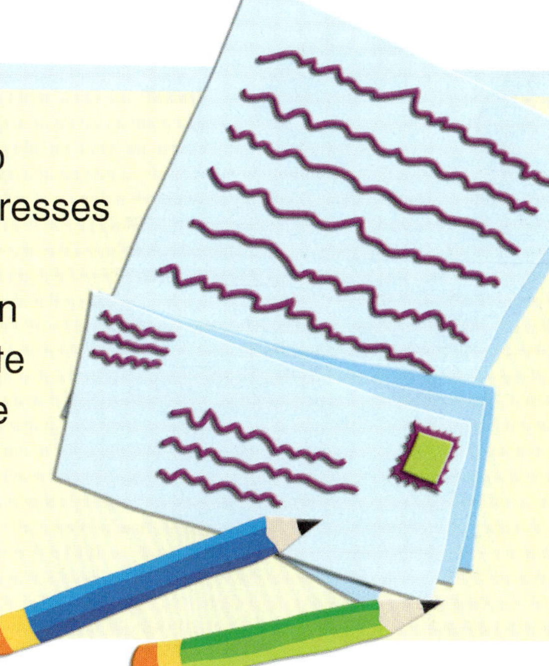

DISCOVER

Catholic Social Teaching

Call to Family, Community, and Participation

Call to Community

God the Father, God the Son, and God the Holy Spirit are a communion of divine love. God made humans to live in community. To teach people how to live in their first community—the family—God sent his own Son to live in a family with Mary and Joseph.

Catholics are called by their faith to participate in family life. The faith also calls Catholics to share life and love with their community. Each time a family member acts with love, the family grows stronger. Each time a person shares in community life, the community grows stronger.

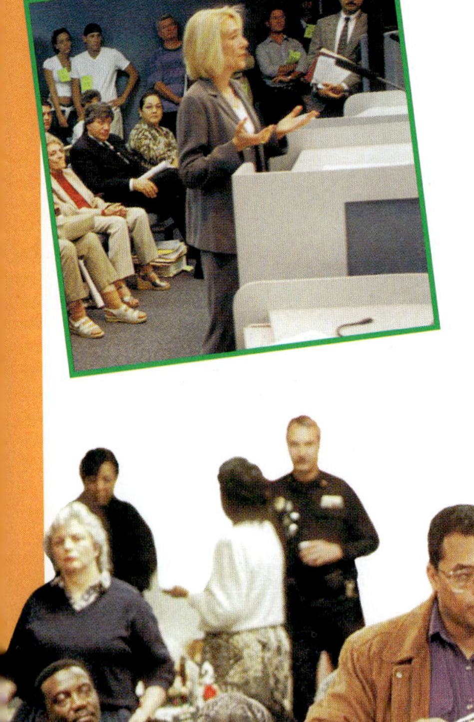

? How can you help your family and your community grow stronger?

CONNECT

With the Call to Justice

Families Helping Families

Let's see what a group of families is doing to answer God's call to family, community, and participation.

The people of Guatemala and the people of the United States share the same hope of seeing their families become stronger. That takes good food and safe housing, good jobs and education, good medical care and healthier living conditions.

Common Hope is an organization founded by a Catholic family in Minnesota. It helps families in Guatemala live happier and healthier lives. In return, the volunteers and sponsors discover how similar their lives are to those of the people of Guatemala.

Volunteers and sponsors understand that it is important for the Guatemalan families to help themselves. Common Hope provides money and goods to end hunger and to educate children. Once the Guatemalan families make better lives, outside help will no longer be needed.

? How are families in the United States and Guatemala part of one community?

Reach Out!

SERVE

Your Community

Think About Communities

Kyle and Bridget are twins in a large family. Because they are the youngest children, the twins think that they have no responsibilities to their family.

What would you tell Kyle and Bridget?

____

____

How might the twins help their family grow stronger?

____

____

The Farrells are new in town. They are all very busy with school and work. They say that they don't have time to get involved in their new community.

How could the Farrells help make their community stronger?

____

____

How could their new community make the Farrell family stronger?

____

____

Make a Difference

Improve Your School Community What would make your school a stronger, better community? Does your playground need cleaning? Does anyone need help with homework? Or maybe your school needs a new computer. Together with your class, decide on one item or service that would help, and plan to make it a reality.

DISCOVER

Catholic Social Teaching:

Option for the Poor and Vulnerable

Option for the Poor

Jesus' actions showed that he loved and cared for people who were poor, sick, or lonely. Your mission is to help others by imitating his loving actions. But who needs your help most? Like Jesus, you are called to help people who are poor.

The Catholic Church teaches its members to be responsible for everyone in need, especially those who are poor. Organized groups, such as the St. Vincent de Paul Society, care for the needs of those who are poor. Individual Catholics give money, volunteer their time, and pray for those in need.

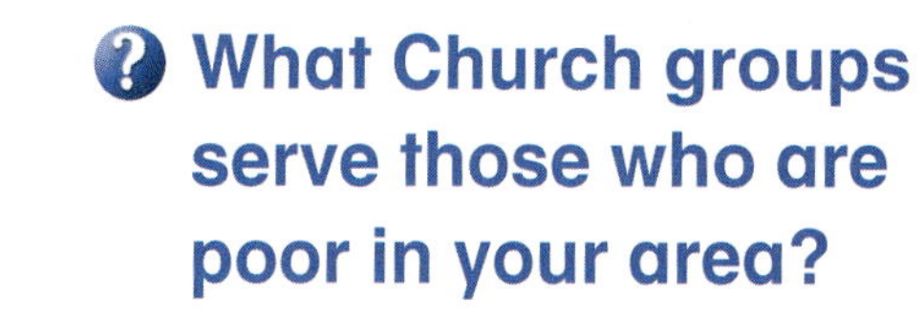

What Church groups serve those who are poor in your area?

CONNECT

With the Call to Justice

Following in Vincent's Footsteps

You are called to care for those around you who are in need. Let's see how one parish is feeding those who are hungry and spreading the message of God's love.

A Catholic church in Illinois is named for Saint Vincent de Paul, a man who became a priest and worked with those who were poor. The parishioners honor their patron saint by serving those who are poor and homeless.

The Sandwich Window and Food Pantry began at St. Vincent's in 1980. Volunteers who run the project serve soup, sandwiches, muffins, and coffee every morning. In one month alone, the parish serves more than 2,000 sandwiches and almost 250 gallons of coffee!

The parishioners discovered that their guests also need to know how much God loves them. Along with soup and sandwiches, extra helpings of hospitality, self-respect, and friendship are served each day. Through the volunteers' love, the guests discover that God loves them.

What else might the parish want to do in the future for those who are poor?

Reach Out!

SERVE

Your Community

Start Helping

You are not too young to help care for those who are poor and others in need. On each sandwich shape below, write one thing you will do to help someone in need during the next month.

Make a Difference

Tell About the Need Many people still do not realize how many people in this country are poor or hungry. As a class, write a letter to the editor of your local newspaper, asking people to help solve the problems of those who are poor and hungry in your area. You might also write a class letter to an elected official, asking that person to pass laws that help those in need in your community, in your country, and throughout the world.

Words of Faith

Anointing of the Sick This sacrament celebrates Jesus' healing of the body and spirit. *(182)*

Apostles The first twelve leaders called by Jesus. *(123)*

authority To have authority is to be in charge of something and have the power to make decisions. *(61)*

Beatitudes Teachings of Jesus that show the way to true happiness and tell how to live in God's kingdom. *(149)*

Bible God's word written in human words. The Bible is the holy book of the Church. *(51)*

bishops Ordained men who work with the pope in teaching and guiding the Church. The bishops are the successors of the Apostles. *(123)*

Blessed Sacrament The Holy Eucharist, especially the blessed Bread that is kept in the tabernacle. *(79)*

Body of Christ A name for the Church of which Christ is the head. All the baptized are members of the body. *(111)*

catholic A word that means "universal" or "everywhere." The Church is meant for all people in all times and all places. *(138)*

chrism The blessed oil used in the Sacraments of Baptism, Confirmation, and Holy Orders. *(173)*

Christians Followers of Jesus Christ. The word "Christian" comes from "Christ." *(201)*

Church The community of the People of God gathered in the name of Jesus Christ. *(53)*

communion of saints Everyone who has been redeemed by Jesus—people on earth, people who have died and are in purgatory, and the saints in heaven. *(131)*

community A group of people who work together for a special reason. *(52)*

conscience A gift from God that helps you know the difference between right and wrong. *(165)*

covenant A sacred promise or agreement between God and humans. *(199)*

create To make something completely new. Only God can create something where nothing existed before. *(43)*

creed A statement of the basic beliefs about God the Father, God the Son, and God the Holy Spirit, and about other teachings of the Church. *(71)*

diocese An area of the Church made up of many parishes and led by a bishop. *(123)*

Easter Vigil Liturgy Celebrated on Holy Saturday evening. New members are welcomed into the Church at the Easter Vigil. *(172)*

faith Belief and trust in God. By faith you believe all that God teaches you through the Church. *(156)*

Gospel A word that means "good news." The gospel message is the good news of God's kingdom and saving love. *(95)*

Gospels The four books in the New Testament that tell the stories of Jesus' life, death, and Resurrection. They are the most important books for the Church because they focus on Jesus. *(95)*

grace God's free and loving gift to humans of his own life and friendship. *(165)*

heaven Being with God forever in happiness. *(217)*

hell Being separated from God forever because of a choice to turn away from him. *(217)*

Holy Orders The sacrament in which a man is ordained to serve Jesus and the Church as a deacon, priest, or bishop. *(190)*

Holy Trinity The name for the three Persons in God. *(69)*

hope The virtue that helps you trust in what God has shown you. *(156)*

intercession Asking for God's help for others. *(87)*

justice The virtue of giving God and others what is their due. *(209)*

kingdom of God God's rule of justice, love, and peace. *(97)*

last judgment When Jesus will come again at the end of time to judge the living and the dead and bring the kingdom of God to its fullness. *(217)*

law of love Jesus' law of love sums up the Ten Commandments and the Beatitudes in one statement: "...Love one another. Just as I have loved you, you also should love one another" *(John 13:34)*. *(149)*

liturgy The community worships and praises God in the Mass and the other sacraments. *(78)*

Matrimony The sacrament that joins a man and a woman in Christian marriage. *(190)*

messiah A Hebrew word that means "anointed." Christians believe that Jesus is the Messiah—the one who has been anointed, or chosen. *(97)*

mission A job or duty that someone takes responsibility for. The Church's mission is to announce the good news of God's kingdom. *(139)*

missionaries People who travel to share Jesus' good news. *(139)*

parables Teaching stories that Jesus used to describe the kingdom of God. *(97)*

Paschal mystery The mystery of Jesus' suffering, death, Resurrection, and Ascension. *(105)*

Passover Jewish feast that recalls and celebrates how God led the Israelites out of slavery from Egypt. *(105)*

peace True unity among people that makes them want to respect one another and keep order. It is the good effect of working for justice. *(209)*

Pentecost The feast that celebrates the coming of the Holy Spirit fifty days after Easter. (131)

petition A request for something you want or need. *(87)*

pope The successor of Saint Peter and bishop of Rome. The pope is the highest teacher and guide in the Church. *(122)*

praise To give honor. You praise someone who is good and holy. *(87)*

prayer Talking and listening to God. It is raising your mind and heart to God. *(85)*

precepts of the Church Some of the basic laws Catholics should follow. *(165)*

purgatory A state of final cleansing before entrance into heaven. *(217)*

respect Paying attention to what people say and treating them the way you would like to be treated. *(45)*

responsibility A duty or a job that you are trusted to do. God gives humans the responsibility of caring for his creation. *(45)*

Resurrection The event of Jesus being raised from death to new life by God the Father through the power of the Holy Spirit. (105)

sacraments Signs that come from Jesus and give grace. *(175)*

Sacraments of Healing Reconciliation and the Anointing of the Sick. In these sacraments, God's forgiveness and healing are given to those suffering physical and spiritual sickness. *(183)*

Sacraments of Initiation Baptism, Confirmation, and Eucharist. They celebrate membership in the Catholic Church. *(175)*

Sacraments of Service Holy Orders and Matrimony. They celebrate people's commitment to serve God and the community. *(191)*

sacrifice To give up something for a greater good. *(103)*

second coming When Jesus will come again to judge the living and the dead. This will bring the kingdom of God to its fullness. *(216)*

sin The deliberate choice to disobey God. When you sin, you hurt your relationship with God and other people. *(165)*

theological virtues Faith, hope, and love, which are gifts from God. *(157)*

virtues Good qualities, or habits of goodness. The theological virtues of faith, hope, and love are gifts from God. *(157)*

Visitation The name of the visit of Mary to Elizabeth. *(59)*

vows Sacred promises that are made to or before God. In marriage a man and a woman make their promises to love each other and to be faithful before God. *(189)*

worship To adore and honor God. *(79)*

Boldfaced numbers refer to pages on which the terms are defined.

Illustration Credits

43 (cr) Gray Glover; 43 (cr) Lori Lohstoeter; 48 (bl) Lois Woolley; 50 (b) Jean Hirashima; 51 (cr) Adam Hook; 53 (br) Judy Stead; 56 (bl) Lois Woolley; 59 (cr) Phil Howe; 64 (bl) Lois Woolley; 67 (b) Gray Glover; 68 (b) Paul Bachem; 69 (b) Paul Bachem; 74 (bl) Lois Woolley 77 (cr) Robert Sauber; 82 (bl) Lois Woolley; 84 (b) Kevin Beilfuss; 89 (br) Judy Stead; 90 (bl) Lois Woolley; 94 (bl) Peter Fiore; 95 (br) Judy Stead; 96 (b) Bill Maughan; 100 (bl) Lois Woolley; 104 (b) Kevin Bielfuss; 105 (br) Judy Stead; 108 (bl) Lois Woolley; 112 (bl) Adam Hook; 115 (br) Judy Stead; 116 (bl) Lois Woolley; 120 (br) Micheal Jaroszko; 121 (tr) Michael Jaroszko; 121 (cr) Michael Jaroszko; 123 (br) Judy Stead; 126 (bl) Lois Woolley; 129 (br) Judy Stead; 130 (b) Jeff Preston; 131 (cr) Jeff Preston; 134 (bl) Lois Woolley; 135 (b) Phil Howe; 136 (bl) Frank Riccio; 137 Judy Stead; 138 (b) Kevin Bielfuss; 142 (bl) Lois Woolley; 146 (cl) Bill Maughan; 146 (bl) Bill Maughan; 147 (cr) Bill Maughan; 148 (b) Michael Jaroszko; 152 (bl) Lois Woolley; 154 (b) Corey Wolfe; 155 (cr) Corey Wolfe; 159 (br) Judy Stead; 160 (bl) Lois Woolley; 162 (bl) Philip Howe; 163 (tr) Mario Capaldi; 164 (c) Judy Stead; 168 (bl) Lois Woolley; 171 (bl) Lori Lohstoeter; 174 (bl) Robert Rodriguez; 175 (br) Judy Stead; 178 (bl) Lois Woolley; 180 (b) Dave Henderson; 181 (tr) Dave Henderson; 183 (b) Judy Stead; 186 (bl) Lois Woolley; 193 (cr) Judy Stead; 194 (bl) Lois Woolley; 198 (b) Jeff Preston; 200 (b) Tom Newsom; 201 (br) Judy Stead; 203 (cr) Judy Stead; 204 (bl) Lois Woolley; 207 (tr) Adam Hook; 209 (br) Judy Stead; 212 (bl) Lois Woolley; 214 (bl) Lori Lohstoeter; 214 (bkgd) Lori Lohstoeter; 219 (bl) Judy Stead; 220 (bl) Lois Woolley

Photo Credits

1 l Rubberball Productions/Getty Images; 1 r Rubberball Productions/Getty Images; 2 Jupiterimages/Getty Images; 6-7 Terry Vine/Riser/Getty Images; 7 inset Father Gene Plaisted, OSC; 10-11 bg Liane Cary/AgeFotostock; 11 c C Squared Studios/Photodisc/Getty Images; 10-11 b Richard Hutchings; 12-13 Father Gene Plaisted, OSC; 14-15 bg Lloyd Sutton/Masterfile; 14-15 fg Felicia Martinez/PhotoEdit; 18-19 bg Thinkstock/Getty Images; 18-19 b A. Ramey/PhotoEdit; 19 inset Father Gene Plaisted, OSC; 22-23 EPA/Piyal Adhikary/AP; 26-27 Richard Hutchings/PhotoEdit; 28-29 Father Gene Plaisted, OSC; 30-31 Photodisc; 34-35 bg J. A. Kraulis/Masterfile; 35 fg Richard Hutchings; 38-39 bg Larry Hirshowitz/CORBIS; 39 inset Stockbyte/Getty Images; 40 l Mark Wetters Images/Getty Images; 40 c Eric Camden; 40 r Walter Hodges/Corbis; 40-41 bg Mark Wetters Images/Getty Images; 42 Ed McDonald; 44 l Ed McDonald; 44 r Rob Gage/Taxi/Getty Images; 45 David Young-Wolff/PhotoEdit; 46 Gabe Palmer/Corbis; 49 fg Eric Camden; 49 bg Eric Camden; 51 Sonny Senser; 52 t Tom & Dee Ann McCarthy/Corbis; 52 b LWA-Dann Tardif/CORBIS; 53 Brand X Pictures/Punchstock; 54 Myrleen Ferguson Kate/PhotoEdit; 56 Eric Camden; 57 Walter Hodges/Corbis; 58 Eric Camden; 60 Sonny Senser; 61 Adam Smith/Taxi/Getty Images; 62 Myrleen Ferguson Cate/PhotoEdit; 66 c Jose Carillo/PhotoEdit; 66 r Cleo Photography/PhotoEdit; 70 t Thinkstock/Comstock Images/Getty Images; 70 b Ken Chernus/The Image Bank/Getty Images; 71 Colorblind/Photodisc/Getty Images; 72 Myrleen Ferguson Cate/PhotoEdit; 74 Ed McDonald; 75 Jose Carillo/PhotoEdit; 76 FK Photo/Corbis; 77 Sonny Senser; 78 l Jim Whitmer Photography; 78 r Father Gene Plaisted, OSC; 79 Bill Wittman; 82 Tom Stewart/Corbis; 83 Cleo Photography/PhotoEdit; 85 Ed McDonald; 86-87 Eric Camden; 88 Myrleen Ferguson Cate/PhotoEdit; 90 Ed McDonald; 92 l Ed McDonald; 92 c Eric Camden; 92 r Kevin Cozad/O'Brien Productions/Corbis; 92-93 bg Ed McDonald; 98 Myrleen Ferguson Cate/PhotoEdit; 101 fg Eric Camden; 101 bg Ryan McVay/Stockbyte/Getty Images; 102 Ed McDonald; 103 Ed McDonald; 106 Jim Whitmer Photography; 108 David Young-Wolff/Stone/Getty Images; 109 Kevin Cozad/O'Brien Productions/Corbis; 110 Eric Camden; 111 Bill Wittman; 113 AFP Photo/Stan Honda/Getty Images; 114 Rubberball Productions/Getty Images; 116 Bill Wittman; 118 l Eric Camden; 118 c Robert Harding Picture Library Ltd/Alamy; 119 Eric Camden; 121 Sonny Senser; 122 Alessandra Benedetti/Corbis; 123 Bill Wittman; 124 Father Gene Plaisted, OSC; 127 Robert Harding Picture Library Ltd/Alamy; 128 Mary Kate Denny/PhotoEdit; 129 t Patrick Robert/Sygma/Corbis; 129 b NASA; 132 cr Walter Wick/Taxi/Getty Images; 132 br Novastock/PhotoEdit; 134 Ariel Skelley/Corbis; 140 Andersen Ross/Photodisc/Getty Images; 144 l Eric Camden; 144 c Adam Woolfitt/Corbis; 144 r LWA-Dann Tardif; 144-145 bg Eric Camden; 147 Ed McDonald; 149 Photodisc/Punchstock; 150 Ed McDonald; 153 Adam Woolfitt/Corbis; 156-157 Sonny Senser; 158 David Toase/PhotoDisc/Getty Images; 160 Eric Camden; 161 LWA-Dann Tardif; 165 Ed McDonald; 166 Myrleen Ferguson Cate/PhotoEdit; 168 Warren Morgan/Corbis; 170 c Ed McDonald; 170 r Ed McDonald; 172 Jack Holtel/Photographik Company; 173 Father Gene Plaisted, OSC; 175 bg Sonny Senser; 175 inset Royalty-Free/Corbis; 176 Eric Camden; 179 Ed McDonald; 181 Ed McDonald; 182 t Jack Holtel/Photographik Company; 182 b Sonny Senser; 183 Jim Whitmer Photography; 184 Myrleen Ferguson Cate/PhotoEdit; 186 Ronnie Kaufman/Corbis; 187 Ed McDonald; 188 t Ed McDonald; 188 b Ed McDonald; 189 Bill Wittman; 190 t Comstock Images/Jupiter Images; 190 b Sonny Senser; 191 Paul Barton/Corbis; 192 Father Gene Plaisted, OSC; 194 Bard Martin/The Image Bank/Getty Images; 196 l plainpicture/Wolfgang Kucher; 196 l Gordon Whitten/Corbis; 196 c Steven Rubin/The Image Works, Inc; 196 r Ed McDonald; 196-197 bg Gordon Whitten/Corbis; 197 fg plainpicture/Wolfgang Kucher; 201 Bill Wittman; 202 David Keaton/Corbis; 204 Ed McDonald; 205 Steven Rubin/The Image Works, Inc; 206 Charles Mistral/Alamy; 207 Sonny Senser; 208 t David Turnley/Corbis; 208 b Stephen Epstein/Ponka Wonka; 209 DESHAKALYAN CHOWDHURY/AFP/Getty Images; 210 Bill Wittman; 213 Ed McDonald; 215 Ed McDonald; 216 Eric Camden; 217 Father Gene Plaisted, OSC; 218 James Brey/Vetta/Getty Images; 220 Ronnie Kaufman/Corbis; 222-223 Richard Hutchings; 225 Father Gene Plaisted, OSC; 226 KAI PFAFFENBACH/Reuters/Corbis; 227 Photos.com; 228 Tohoku Color Agency/Japan Images/Getty Images; 229 Father Gene Plaisted, OSC; 230 t Father John Guiliani/Bridge Building Images; 230 b Bill Wittman; 232 Photodisc/Getty Images; 233 t Digital Imaging Group; 233 c Digital Imaging Group; 233 b Digital Imaging Group; 235 Clark Dunbar/Corbis; 236 Myrleen Ferguson Cate/PhotoEdit; 237 BananaStock/BananaStock, Ltd./PictureQuest; 238-239 Thinkstock/Getty Images; 240-241 Thinkstock/Getty Images; 242-243 Thinkstock/Getty Images; 244-245 Thinkstock/Getty Images; 246-247 Thinkstock/Getty Images; 248-249 Thinkstock/Getty Images; 250 l Guy Cali/Corbis; 250 l SW Productions/PhotoDisc/Getty Images; 250 l Jeff Greenberg/Photo Edit; 250 l Michael Newman/Photo Edit; 250 l Myrleen Ferguson Cate/PhotoEdit; 250 l Common Hope; 250 l Myrleen Ferguson Cate/PhotoEdit; 251 t Reed Kaestner/Corbis; 251 b Guy Cali/Corbis; 252 t Zane Williams/Stone/Getty Images; 252 b Terry Vine/Stone/Getty Images; 253 Antony Edwards/Image Bank/Getty Images; 254 t Bill Aron/PhotoEdit; 254 c Patrik Giardino/Corbis; 254 b Michael A. Dwyer/Stock Boston; 255 c St. Joseph Church; 255 bl SW Productions/PhotoDisc/Getty Images; 255 br Travelpix Ltd/Getty Images; 256 c Eric Camden; 256 b Travelpix Ltd/Getty Images; 257 t Mark Richards/Photo Edit; 257 b Jeff Greenberg/Photo Edit; 258 bl Courtesy of Nazareth Farm; 258 bc David Young-Wolff/PhotoEdit; 258 br Aneal Vohra/Index Stock Imagery/Photolibrary; 260 t Sondra Dawes/The Image Works, Inc.; 260 b Michael Newman/Photo Edit; 260-261 bg Design Pics/JupiterImages; 261 t Peter Hvizdak/The Image Works, Inc.; 261 b Michael Newman/Photo Edit; 262 Design Pics/JupiterImages; 263 t Kevin Anthony Horgan/Image Bank/Getty Images; 263 b Bill Aron/PhotoEdit; 264 bl Myrleen Ferguson Cate/PhotoEdit; 264 br Pascal Le Segretain/Sygma/Corbis; 266 t Jeff Greenberg/PhotoEdit; 266 b Bob Daemmrich/The Image Works, Inc.; 267cl Common Hope; 267 bl Common Hope; 267 br Antony Nagelmann/Taxi/Getty Images; 268 c Imagemore/SuperStock; 268 b Antony Nagelmann/Taxi/Getty Images; 269 fg Greg Smith/CORBIS SABA; 269 bg Mark Ludak/The Image Works, Inc.; 270 c Myrleen Ferguson Cate/PhotoEdit; 270 b Don Smetzer/PhotoEdit; 271 Don Smetzer/PhotoEdit

Acknowledgments

For permission to reprint copyrighted material, grateful acknowledgment is made to the following sources:

OCP Publications, 5536 NE Hassalo, Portland, OR 97213: Lyrics from "Veni, Sancte, Spiritus" by Christopher Walker. Lyrics © 1981, 1982 by Christopher Walker. Lyrics from "Glory to God" by Dan Schutte. Lyrics © by Daniel L. Schutte. All rights reserved.

Patricia Joyce Shelly: Lyrics from "All Grownups, All Children" by Patricia Joyce Shelly. Lyrics © 1977 by Patricia Joyce Shelly.

Twenty-Third Publications, A Division of Bayard: "Grace Before Meals" (Retitled: "Grace Before Mealtime"), "Grace After Meals" (Retitled: "Grace After Mealtime"), and "Morning Offering" from *500 Prayers for Catholic Schools & Parish Youth Groups* by Filomena Tassi and Peter Tassi. Text copyright © 2004 by Filomena Tassi and Peter Tassi.

United States Conference of Catholic Bishops, Inc., Washington, D.C.: From the English translation of "Blessing on Birthdays or the Anniversary of Baptism" (Retitled: "Prayer of Blessing for a Child's Birthday") in *Book of Blessings.* Translation copyright © 1988 by United States Catholic Conference, Inc. From the English translation of "At Bedside" (Retitled: "Evening Prayer") from *Catholic Household Blessings and Prayers.* Translation copyright © 1989 by United States Catholic Conference, Inc.